AF469688

WAY OF THE GAMEKEEPER

OTHER TITLES AVAILABLE

The Notorious Poacher
G. Bedson ("Grandad")

Shotgun Shooting
Dr. John Brindle

Ratting and Rabbiting
Guy N. Smith

The Pheasants of the World
Dr. J. Delacour

Gamekeeping and Shooting for Amateurs
Guy N. Smith

Cockfighting and Game Fowl
Herbert Atkinson

Guinea Fowl of the World
R. H. Hastings Belshaw

Advanced Taxidermy
P. A. O'Connor

WAY
OF
THE GAMEKEEPER

by

JILL MASON

Distributor:
Nimrod Book Services
PO Box 1
Liss, Hants, GU33 7PR
England

ISBN 086230 063 0

Publisher:
NIMROD BOOK SERVICES
Fanciers Supplies Ltd
P.O. Box 1
Liss, Hants, GU33 7PR

S & R Printers Ltd., 236 Balham High Road, London SW17 7AW

CONTENTS

Chapter   *Page*
    List of Illustrations   *vi*
    Author's Preface   *viii*
    Editor's Introduction   *x*
1. Gamekeeping To-day   1
2. John Starts His Career — February   9
3. The First Snow — March   29
4. The Laying Season — April   39
5. Rearing Preparations — May   55
6. The Growing Season — June   73
7. The Game Fair — July   83
8. Dealing With The Elements — August   97
9. The Tidying-up Month — September   109
10. Counting And Planning — October   123
11. The Shooting Season Begins — November   137
12. Season Of Goodwill — December   161
13. A Special Shoot — January   175
14. The Season Ends   181

LIST OF ILLUSTRATIONS

Figure		*Page*
1.	A Gamekeeper of Old	ix
2.	Plan of the Estate	xviii
1.1	The Pointer at Work	2
1.2	Large Houses and Estates all had Gamekeepers	5
1.3	Shooting Parties were Commonplace	6
2.1	Gamekeeping 160 Years Ago	10
2.2	Laying Birds in Pen	13
2.3	An Overgrown Pond	15
2.4	A Roe Deer Emerged	17
2.5	Brail in Position (inside)	25
2.6	Brail in Position (outside)	26
2.7	Winter in the Woods	28
3.1	The Snow-covered Landscape	30
3.2	A Fox Snare in Position	32
3.3	Tunnel with Fenn Trap Inside	33
3.4	Fenn Trap in Set Position	34
3.5	Western Incubator filled with Eggs	36
3.6	Weasels with a Bird Victim	38
4.1	The Poacher Fox	40
4.2	The Villain is Dead	42
4.3	A Labrador Puppy	45
4.4	Pheasants Eggs Laid under Fir Boughs in Laying Pen	49
4.5	Remains of Pheasants and Rabbits Round the Entrance of a Fox Earth	50
4.6	The Plucky Terrier	51
4.7	Getting the Eggs Ready	53
4.8	Various Types of Rearing Coop and Carrying Box (Based on old-style designs)	54
5.1	Sitting Boxes and Broody Hens Releasing Young Poults	56
5.2	Getting the Equipment Ready	58
5.3	A Hen Sitting	60
5.4	Hatching	62
5.5	Egg Trays after Hatching	65
5.6	Chicks Ready to be Moved	66
5.7	Chicks at Three Days Old on Grass	68

5.8	De-beaking in Progress	70
5.9	Melanistic Chick 'They Look Like Magpies'	72
6.1	The Woods in the Growing Season	74
6.2	Poult at Three Weeks Old fitted with Plastic Bit	76
6.3	View of Modern Rearing Field	78
6.4	Top of Gas Cylinder Showing Regulator and Heater	81
7.1	Game Fair: Dog Trial Finals	84
7.2	Healthy Poults at Six Weeks	87
7.3	Feather Picking Illustrated	89
7.4	Goshawks are a Feature of the Game Fair	94
8.1	Friend or Foe?	98
8.2	Type of Pheasant Food	100
8.3	A Strip of Artichokes which provide Excellent Cover	105
8.4	Jill Mason with Bob, Badger and Meg	108
9.1	A Poult eating Greenstuff	110
9.2	Sally Training	114
9.3	Skinned Roe Deer	116
9.4	Pigeon Decoys in Position	118
9.5	The Majestic Pheasant	122
10.1	A Brown Hare Relaxes	124
10.2	Dreaming of Old Time Keeping	130
10.3	Gun Stands (Sticks or Pegs)	131
10.4	Sewelling	134
10.5	A Shooting Party at Wilton Long Ago	136
11.1	Rabbits Coming Out to Feed	138
11.2	Assembly Before the Shoot	142
11.3	Pheasant Shooting: Beaters Walking through Kale	145
11.4	The Game Larder at the End of the Day	147
11.5	Sussex Shoot in the Rain	152
11.6	Snapshot Over the Hedge	155
11.7	At the End of the Day	157
11.8	A Shadow Dance	160
12.1	The Shoot Is On	162
12.2	The German Shepherd Dog (Alsatian) used as a Guard Dog	165
12.3	12-Bore Shotgun and Cartridges	166
12.4	A Poacher at Bay	174
13.1	The Author when the Shoot is Over	176
13.2	Winter Feed Ride	178
14.1	On the Alert	182
14.2	Old Man's Beard Amongst Yew and Silver Birch	186
14.3	The Old Hurdle Maker — a Dying Breed	187
14.4	The Pub from an Old Scene	189

AUTHOR'S PREFACE

A few years ago my husband, David, advertised for a trainee keeper on the estate where we both worked and it was reading through the two hundred and seventy replies which he received that I realised how little most of the applicants knew of what was involved in the day to day running of a pheasant shoot. Since then I have endeavoured to write a book that youngsters and perhaps the not quite so young would find both interesting and informative about keepering. The characters are fictional, but the events are based on fact and could all happen to any keeper in the course of a year.

Jill Mason

ACKNOWLEDGEMENTS

Carter News Agency, Pamela Harrison, Frank H. Meads, Roy Shaw, John Tarlton, Chas White, Robin Williams.

Figure 1   A Gamekeeper of Old

EDITOR'S INTRODUCTION

Gamekeeping has a long history, closely associated with country life and rural sports. Naturally, the function has always been linked with estates, lords of the manor and land owners. In recent times, with rising costs, syndicates of businessmen have come to the rescue, paying considerable sums to keep shoots in existence.

An earlier work *(The Sportsman's Dictionary,* 1778) defines a gamekeeper in the following terms:

> **"GAMEKEEPERS, are those who have the care of keeping and preserving the game, and are appointed to that office by lords of manors, etc. who not being under the degree of esquire, may by a writing, under their hands and seals, authorize one or more gamekeepers, who may seize guns, dogs, or nets used by unqualified persons for destroying the game. Gamekeepers are also to be persons either qualified by law to kill the game, or to be truly and properly the servants of the lords or ladies of manors appointing them; and no gamekeepers can qualify any person to such end, or to keep dogs, etc. as may be seen by the several game acts.**
>
> **The persons qualified to keep guns, dogs, etc. are those who have a free warren, £100 a year by inheritance, or for life, or a lease for 99 years of £150 per annum also the eldest sons of esquires, etc. A lord of manor may appoint a gamekeeper within his manor and royalty to kill hares, pheasants, partridges, etc. for his own use, the name of whom is to be entered with the clerk of the peace of the country; and if any other gamekeeper, or one illegally authorized, under colour of his authority, kills game, and afterwards sells it, without the consent of the person that impowers him, he is conviction to suffer corporal punishment."**

The hours are long and arduous and, therefore, gamekeeping is only for those who are prepared to work long hours. Moreover, quite often, there is still a clear distinction made between those who shoot (the 'guns') and those who rear the game and serve on the estates. Such social distinction may seem to some a relic of bygone days with no place in the twentieth century. Others who have chosen gamekeeping as a career accept the position because it gives them a freedom and outdoor life which is not to be found in many other occupations.

Undoubtedly, we all dream of turning to nature and enjoying the woods, grass, flowers, rivers and many other aspects of country life. The wild life is an integral part of any rural activities and therefore, the work of the gamekeeper or those who toil on the land affect all who enjoy the countryside.

This somewhat romantic approach still exists — and why not? At the other extreme, the anti-Field Sports fraternity quite wrongly assume that gamekeeping is concerned only with killing. Yet from quite early times it has been recognized that a gamekeeper's role was primarily to *protect* and to *conserve*. This is still the position to-day — the control of vermin and the preservation of game are still the main concern of the modern gamekeeper.

Jill Mason is married to a gamekeeper and is also a gamekeeper in her own right. Her factual account is a concise, interesting and human story which sketches the present-day activities of rearing pheasants, organizing a shoot and dealing with the predators of game.

From childhood many boys (and even girls) look upon country sports as delightful pursuits as evidenced by the following poem *(British Field Sports,* William Henry Scott, 1820):

THE

Sportsman's Progress.

When I was but a little boy,
And scarce could lift a Gun,
I oft would leave each childish toy,
And to the fields would run.
With Pistol for my Fowling-piece,
I thought myself a man,
And thus improving by degrees,
A Sportsman's life began.
On Lark and Redwing and Fieldfare,
My skill I first did try,
At every bird that wings the air
I quickly would let fly:
And thus did I in early life,
Each vice and folly shun,
Preferring still, to scenes of strife,
My faithful Dog and Gun.

When older grown, a Gun I got,
A Pointer too I bought,
And being now a decent shot,
The stubble field I sought:
Where, 'neath the weeds bedeck'd with dew,
The cow'ring covey lies,
Till startled by my Pointer true,
To seek the covert flies:
Save one, which in its whirring flight,
The death fraught shot o'ertakes,
And welcome falling in my sight,
A joyful trophy makes.
And thus did I in early life,
Each vice and folly shun,
Preferring still, to scenes of strife,
My faithful Dog and Gun.

With Setters and with Spaniels too,
The woods I rang'd around,
And if a Pheasant came in view,
I brought it to the ground.
And often would I take my way
O'er wastes which ne'er were till'd,
Where in the warren Rabbits play,
Full many a one I kill'd.
And if by chance a good fat Hare
Up from the furzes got,
My Fowling-piece I levell'd fair,
And seldom miss'd a shot.
And thus did I in early life,
Each vice and folly shun,
Preferring still to scenes of strife,
My faithful Dog and Gun.

Sometimes I sought the upland moor,
And rocks with heather crown'd,
Where Black and Red Grouse, both good store,
And Ptarmigan abound:
Or where, thro' woods, all shaded lies
The channel of the brook,
At Snipes and Woodcocks in their rise
My certain aim I took:
Or if by chance I bent my way
By waters deep and still,
The Heron seeking for its prey,
I seldom failed to kill.
And thus did I in early life,
Each vice and folly shun,
Preferring still to scenes of strife,
My faithful Dog and Gun.

XV

Or by the sedgy stream I steal,
And various wild-fowl shoot,
The Widgeon, Wild-goose, Duck, and Teal,
The Water-hen and Coot:
The Plover too that haunts the moor,
The Bittern in the reeds,
The Curlew on the lone sea-shore,
The Rail that loves the weeds;
The Sea-Lark and the Dotteril,
The Ruff and Reeve and Knot,
The Whimbrel with its bending bill,
By river sides I shot.
And thus did I in early life,
Each vice and folly shun,
Preferring still to scenes of strife,
My faithful Dog and Gun.

And thus I lead an easy life,
And ev'ry folly shun,
My joys devoid of care and strife,
Are in my Dog and Gun.
At morn I rise with early dawn,
And to the woods resort,
Or range the stubble or the lawn,
To seek my favourite sport:
And when at eve I homewards pass,
To meet my wife and friends,
I count my spoils and drink my glass,
Till night our pleasure ends:
And still will I thro' all my life,
Each vice and folly shun,
Preferring still to scenes of strife,
My faithful Dog and Gun.

xvii

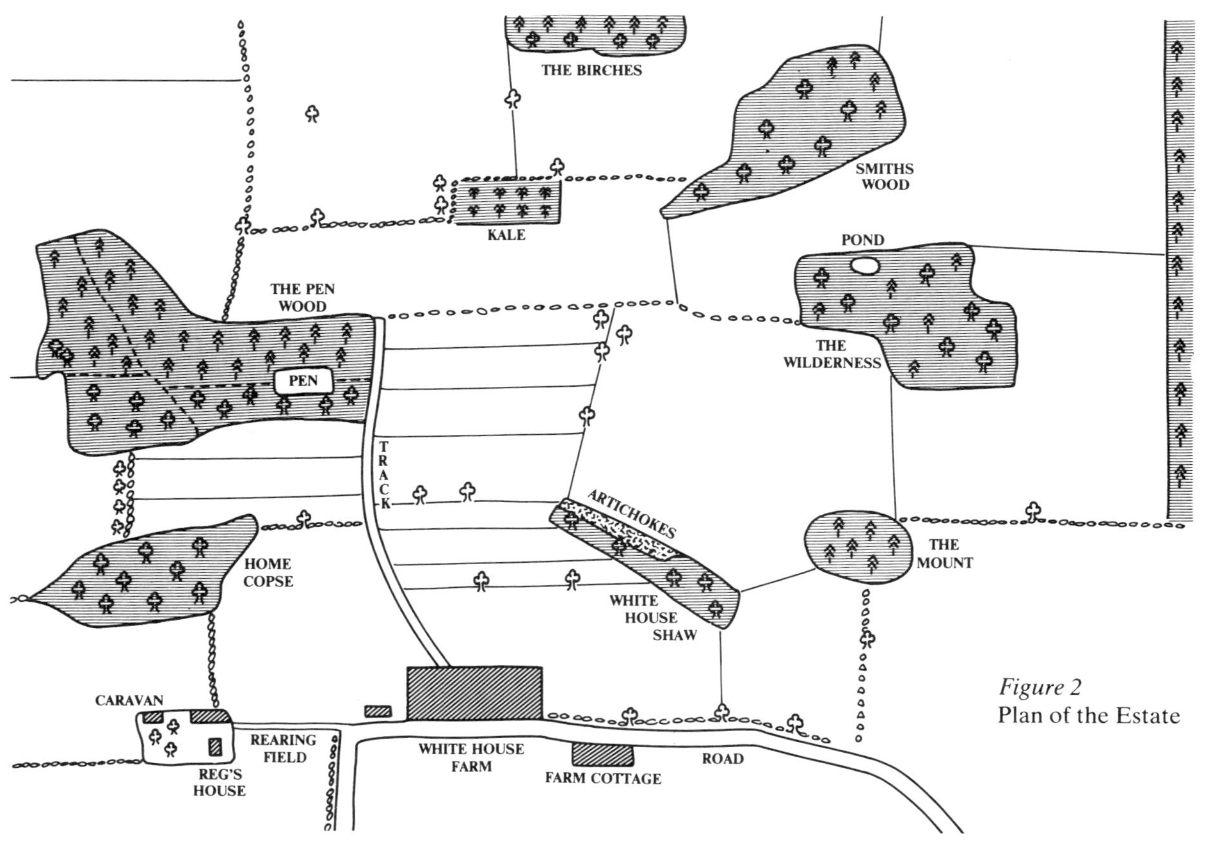

Figure 2
Plan of the Estate

Gamekeeping
Today
1

Figure 1.1. The Pointer at Work

GAMEKEEPING TODAY

PAST AND PRESENT

BRIEF HISTORY

Since man first walked the earth he has hunted; at first it was necessary in order to feed himself. When this was no longer so vital he hunted for his own pleasure. The wealthy kept horses, dogs and hawks to pursue their quarry and employed servants to care for them.

Centuries passed and the muzzle loader was invented introducing a new aspect to hunting; birds could be shot in flight and the sporting potential soon became obvious.

Early shooting

Early shooting was generally confined to walking up game. Dogs, mainly pointers and setters, were used extensively to locate the game. They were trained to mark its position until the guns drew near enough to shoot, then the signal was given to the dogs to flush their quarry. In the lowlands the partridge was the usual object of pursuit, but during the mid-eighteen hundreds, in that mecca of game shooting — East Anglia — a new innovation was conceived, driving pheasants from the woods using a team of men as beaters towards standing guns.

Around this time the safer and far more convenient breech loading gun was produced and the face of shooting changed completely, and driven game over standing guns soon became popular.

Thousands of pheasants were hand-reared with broody hens, their food was mixed from the finest ingredients and they were tended with great care. Estates were carefully planned for sport, woods were planted from which to drive the birds, cover crops were grown and the whole estate revolved around shooting. Rough ground was bounded by banks or wire netting and formed great rabbit warrens providing both sport and food. The head keeper was a very important person, sometimes having his own domestic servants and overseeing vast numbers of beat keepers, under-keepers, warreners and others employed by the estate's Game Department. The English countryside changed and was cherished and preserved.

The Edwardian era was the peak of game shooting, great estates reared and shot thousands of pheasants, they safeguarded the habitat of the wild stock, and game flourished. Shooting was for the wealthy, for Kings and Princes and Lords. There would sometimes be as many as one hundred beaters employed on a shoot day, each dressed in a smock. The head keeper may well have ridden a pony from which he conducted the beaters as a General would an army, and he may well have ended the day with a few gold sovereigns in his pocket given to him by the appreciative guns.

Developments

The 1930's saw a dramatic change. Gone was the euphoria of big shoot days, the production of food not sport became the prime purpose of estates, and farming came to the fore. The advent of World War II drastically increased the need for food and also for timber. Many woods were felled and turned into fields, wire netting from the warrens was ripped up, the young men were set to work on the farms or sent to war. A very few were left to cope, no rearing could be attempted, and wild stock was decimated by uncontrolled vermin and the attentions of soldiers encamped throughout the countryside. Large tracts of land were used as air fields, woods were used as bomb dumps.

Rearing and shooting resumed gradually in the 1950's but farming policies had radically changed the methods of gamekeeping. The Edwardian keepers were now old men and found it difficult to adapt. Modern incubators replaced the broody hen and the pheasant food was delivered in bags.

Many estates were divided up and money could not be spared for the luxury of shooting. Syndicates of paying guns were formed to share the expense and staff was kept to a minimum. Shooting was no longer the sport of the rich, it was made available to a far wider range of men.

Recent history

In recent times another important change to the shooting scene occurred — commercialism. At present many estates are once again increasing their rearing programmes, but now it is to recoup the expenditure or even make a profit from their shooting, by selling several days' shooting during the season to parties of eight or more guns, few of which appreciate the once hallowed etiquette of bygone days. Increasing numbers of foreigners come to Britain to shoot and such goings on would surely make many an old head keeper turn in his grave.

Figure 1.2   Large Houses and Estates all had Gamekeepers

Figure 1.3   Shooting Parties were Commonplace

THE GAMEKEEPER

The present day role of a gamekeeper is to be a jack of all trades, able to turn his hand to anything. No longer the most important employee on the estate he is often a thorn in everyone's side. Farming and pheasant interests rarely coincide and frequently the gamekeeper is employed by one or more persons who neither own or farm the land but just pay for the shooting rights, often leading to little sympathy being shared between the farm staff and the keeper.

Ideally the keeper must be honest, hardworking and diplomatic but many fall far short of these three basic qualifications. The few who possess these qualities are seldom shown any appreciation. Although modern methods of rearing and transport should have eased the work load, much more is expected of the keeper in present times and fewer and fewer men are employed to do the same amount of work. Twenty-five years ago young lads were frequently taken on to train under the existing keeper. This was brought to an end when the powers that be decreed that school leavers should receive a man's wage for doing boys' work. The recent job creation scheme and youth opportunities programme have brought a further decline to young lads being given permanent employment. These latter schemes make available cheap and dispensible labour, youngsters often being taken on for busy summer months and seldom kept on for the rest of the season. It seems a cruel and heartless situation, but to the man in charge of the purse strings it is an ideal answer to his labour problems.

Very few trainee keepers are being taken on at present and in a few years time there may well be a shortage of experienced skilled men, that is if there is still a keepering profession. Should the misguided antis have their own way they would end all blood sports and with the ban would go thousands of jobs and the mass destruction of working dogs and horses. The face of the countryside would drastically change as much of the woodland preserved at present for sport would be of no value either to agriculture or forestry and would be felled.

Gamekeeping as a profession is hovering on the brink of an uncertain future. Apart from the threat from the *antis* the financial burdens are enormous. Sky-high rents are being asked for, and paid; wages, feed bills and general running costs are rising rapidly, while the price paid for dead game is falling due to lack of demand. The net result is that the cost of producing a pheasant that flies over the guns is approximately six times more than its value when it is loaded into the back of the game dealer's van next morning. Few shoot owners can afford this differential; thus the forming of syndicates and the present day trend to letting days.

Future prospects

Prospects for youngsters wishing to gain employment as keepers are very bleak, although help is offered in various ways in the form of advice and practical courses. The Game Conservancy at Fordingbridge, Hampshire offer both, the British Association for Shooting and Conservation based at Rossett, Clwyd, run a placement scheme for their young members whereby they spend three different weeks of the year with a keeper, when they can become familiar with the seasonal routines. Hampshire College of Agriculture at Sparsholt offers a year long course covering gamekeeping and river keeping and other short courses are sometimes advertised, but it must be remembered that there is no guarantee that a job will be available for those who have attended these courses. There are few opportunities and vacancies are rarely advertised. For women the chances are remote; the few that are employed as keepers, albeit usually part time, have generally achieved their position by assisting either their fathers or husbands.

The future for all field sports is uncertain, perhaps the few youngsters entering into employment at present will be the last generation to do so. If this should come to be then this beautiful country of ours will be much the worse for it.

The large estates, with their mansions and parks did not just happen, they were carefully planned by our forefathers to give pleasure and good sport, for which they were willing to meet the expense of such enjoyment, but what the future holds when that pleasure may be put beyond reach cannot be foreseen.

John Starts
His Career
2

FEBRUARY

Figure 2.1 Gamekeeping 160 Years Ago

JOHN STARTS HIS CAREER

MONTH: **FEBRUARY**

MORNING CALL

John woke up feeling warm and cosy, wrapped up in the bedclothes. He was about to snuggle down in bed again when there was a loud banging on the caravan door; he nearly jumped out of his skin.

"Come on — you ought to be up and outside by now," shouted Reg Plummer the Head Keeper impatiently.

"Yes Mr. Plummer — I'm getting up," John assured him tumbling out of bed, trying unsuccessfully to pull his shirt on at the same time as he took off his pyjamas. He had hoped that he had made a good impression so far but oversleeping had ruined that.

JOB-HUNTING

John had left school six months previously and had been serving petrol at a garage during that time, as it was the only work he could find. He had always wanted to be a keeper and had written away for numerous jobs that he had seen advertised only to be told that the vacancy had been filled or that they wanted somebody older and experienced. Many had not even answered his letters so he counted himself very lucky when Mr. Brinklow had taken him on as a trainee keeper at Stonelands. He had already been for one interview for a job at another estate in the Midlands, but they told him they wanted somebody older who could drive, so when John received the summons to attend an interview with Mr. Brinklow and his head keeper at Stonelands, John had felt very sceptical about being offered the job.

The interview

He duly arrived at the appointed time at the big house and was met by Reg Plummer who took him on a quick tour of the estate in the landrover. Reg explained what was involved and what would be required of him. The tour was followed by a brief interview with Mr. Brinklow. After a nerve racking wait in the kitchen Reg had come into the room and asked him when he would be able to start.

For many years John had hoped to be a keeper; he had helped Tom the old keeper near his home and been beating whenever he had the chance and he had enjoyed the occasional visits to his uncle who was a keeper on the Scottish borders, but these visits were few and far between. John was disappointed that he was unable to get a job near his home, but it was extremely difficult to get a start in keepering and he had not hesitated to move to Sussex when he was offered the opportunity.

Accommodation

The living arrangements were not ideal, but as his dad often said 'beggars can't be choosers'. Mrs. Plummer had offered to cook him a midday meal each day and he was to live in a caravan which was parked at the back of Reg Plummer's house on the far side of the orchard. Mrs. Plummer would also do his washing and buy his shopping each week, but it would be up to him to keep the caravan clean. The caravan itself appeared quite comfortable; it was large and had a separate bedroom and shower. There was electricity and water laid on, a gas fire and a small cooker.

BEGINNING WORK

The first two days after he had started work he had got up punctually at a quarter to seven and had plenty of time to cook himself some breakfast before meeting up with Reg at half past. The first day Reg had shown him round the two and a half thousand acre estate, showing him where the release pens were sited and taking him round the woods. Most of the estate was farmed by Mr. Brinklow but about five hundred acres were farmed by a tenant, Mr. Richards. Mr. Brinklow had retained the shooting rights so it made little difference to Reg that the farm was let off. A fair proportion of the estate was wooded and several plantations of fir had been planted during the last twenty five years. The rest of the estate maintained three dairy herds, the progeny of which were reared either as replacements for the herd or to be fattened for beef. The remainder of the land was used to grow cereals.

The Beat

The second day Reg had taken him round the beat that he was to care for. He showed him the feed rides where he was to feed and took him round every wood. As they walked along Reg explained in detail what John should do and how much corn he should feed. He asked him several questions, no

Figure 2.2   Laying Birds in Pen

doubt trying to discover how much John had learned from old Tom and his uncle.

John could easily see where to feed as the leaves were scratched up. Where there was wet mud on the track he could see the footprints of pheasants, but he barely saw one pheasant as they walked along talking.

The pen wood had a large pen in it, where the young pheasant poults had been released the previous summer, and there was a belt of trees that Reg had called a "shaw" with a strip of dried-up looking sticks beside it. John enquired what this was and Reg explained that they were artichokes planted to make the belt wider with enough cover to make an extra drive on a shoot day. In the spring they grew green, and by the end of the summer would be up to seven feet tall and provided good cover. The pheasants also enjoyed pecking at the roots and John could see where some half eaten potato-like roots were showing through the soil.

Reg pointed to a wood in the distance that he had stopped feeding when they had finished shooting — this was called the birches and was near the boundary. This left John six other places to feed and he had carefully listened to Reg's instructions as he was determined to do things right. Reg had told him that he could take the single barrelled **four-ten** that his uncle had given him when he went round and he would get him a few cartridges for it.

Black Mark

Now it was a quarter to eight and he was rushing to get his clothes on, and the first black mark against him was written in Reg's book. John gulped down a large bowlful of cereal and a cup of coffee, it was cold and damp outside and barely light. He tried to creep out of the caravan unobtrusively but when he had gone a hundred yards across the field he remembered his feed bag and foolishly he returned to the shed where it was hanging on a nail amidst the paraphernalia that Reg had accumulated during the fifteen years that he had been at Stonelands. John half filled the bag with wheat from the big corn bin that stood in the corner and set off again across the ploughed field. The place did not seem nearly so attractive as it had in yesterday's sunshine. It was pointless to hurry, and, although there was a well trodden path from the orchard to the first wood, Home Copse, it was very sticky and the clay clung to his boots making them heavy and every step an effort; his legs ached and he realised how unfit he was.

Feeding

He could see the pheasants searching for food along the ride as he neared the wood. He tried to whistle as Reg had showed him, but it didn't sound much like Reg had. Nevertheless the pheasants came running towards him and hungrily ate the grains that he scattered along the ride. There was very little natural food available for the birds in February; the acorns and beech masts had long since been consumed by various birds and animals, the ground was too wet for the spring corn to have been drilled, and the weather too cold for insect life. John threw several handfuls of wheat under the wire netting cages that would be used to catch the birds which would be needed for the laying pen. At present they were propped up on the sticks in each corner so that the pheasants could move freely underneath and get used to them. Reg hoped to soon start catching the pheasants that would be needed to produce enough chicks for the season's rearing programme.

John stood quietly at the end of the ride counting the pheasants that were feeding and waiting to see if any more would emerge from the brambles and dead bracken. He turned and walked out of the wood and along the edge of a grass field which had been divided into paddocks with barbed wire fences which John found difficult to negotiate with his feed bag and bulky clothing.

He reached the wood, which was a half fir plantation and half oak and hazel, where the pen was. He walked along the track and took the right hand fork that led to the pen. One side of the track was the plantation, thick and dark. A carpet of dry needles covered the ground beneath. Reg had told him that it had been planted only a few years before he had started at Stonelands and now it was tall enough to walk silently underneath. The other side of the track were great oak trees with hazel bushes growing below; patches of bracken and brambles grew where sufficient light could penetrate. The pen was built half in the plantation and half in the high wood: John fed along the track that divided the two halves, and underneath the four catchers that were placed along the feed ride. He waited at the end of the ride half hidden by a big oak.

The pheasants seemed more timid here, some nervously crept out onto the ride and once they started to feed others hastily joined them. John waited patiently until no more came. There were more hens than cocks and it was difficult to count them as the hens darted to and fro. If two cocks came close together there was a skirmish, with one soon turning tail and disappearing back into the cover only to reappear a few yards away a moment later. John watched fascinated as blackbirds and robins joined in the free meal and two squirrels climbed hesitatingly down a tree and began to search through the leaves for the corn. Higher in the trees blue tits, great tits and long tailed tits flew from branch to branch. A jay flipped down to the ground amongst the pheasants, but a slight movement from John soon sent it back into the trees. John watched them all with interest; it had never occurred to him how many other birds and animals would benefit from the pheasants being fed.

Smiths

After several minutes not wishing to disturb the creatures, he crept quietly away. He continued along the track and climbed over the rails out

Figure 2.3   An Overgrown Pond

into the field of winter wheat. He walked across the corner of the field and climbed through a gap in the hedge. On his left was the wood called the Birches, which was a large fir plantation flanked by a row of silver birch. Being on the boundary Reg had stopped feeding and hoped that the pheasants would draw back into the middle of the shoot, making them easier to catch up. By-passing the birches John continued his way across a grass field to another wood called Smiths. This was a large block of oak and hazel with a small plantation which had been planted five years previously – between the rows of head-high Christmas trees was a tangle of grass, birch and brambles. He fed along the path that had been trimmed through the hazel and continued on his way across another grass field to a big wood known as Wilderness. He passed through the gate into the wood and he saw on his left an overgrown pond. Willows grew round the banks and the remains of once stately bulrushes littered one side of the pond. A moorhen paddled across the water and found cover in the bulrushes and a pair of teal sprung from the water and sought safety in the sky. Behind the willows higher up on the bank stood two ancient yew trees; by their size they must have been hundreds of years old and John wondered at the changes in their surroundings they must have witnessed since they first took root and grew.

Wilderness

He walked on through the wood discovering why it had been named Wilderness. Besides the usual oak and hazel was a wide variety of trees and shrubs; great beech trees, birch, cherry trees and a huge sweet chesnut its trunk gnarled and twisted and almost hollow. Beneath the taller trees grew brambles, holly and rhododendrons. He scattered the grain along the well scratched feed ride that ran diagonally through the wood and climbed over the gate out of the wood and into the field that had last grown kale.

The cows had long finished eating it and now the field was a quagmire, hoof prints several inches deep lay half filled with muddy water — he tried to pick his way through but invariably his feet slipped into the holes and the muddy waters squirted up his legs making him wish he had put his leggings on instead of leaving in such a hurry. The earlier drizzle had turned to rain and the water dripped off his coat, his jeans clung to his legs and the inside of his wellingtons felter wetter and wetter as they filled.

The Mount

The next place he fed was a circular clump of tall scotch pine trees called the Mount. Brambles grew profusely underneath, but in the middle was a clearing covered with a thick layer of pine needles. It was like an expensive carpet to walk on, and where the pheasants had been fed it was well

Figure 2.4   A Roe Deer Emerged

scratched. He scattered the corn along the ride and underneath the catchers and walked along the narrow path through the brambles that led to the surrounding fence. He leaped across the ditch on the edge of the trees and slipped on the far bank; he grabbed at the fence, but not quick enough to prevent him sliding into the bottom of the ditch, the water seeped over the top of one of his wellngtons: it felt icy cold. He scrambled out of the ditch and under the fence, and inspected the damage to the finger that he had ripped on the barbed wire when he had grabbed at it. The blood mingled with the dirt on his hand and he thought it better to let it bleed to wash the dirt out of the cut. He leaned against the fence post and withdrew his foot from his wellington. The water was muddy and full of rotten leaves when he tipped it out of his boot and wrung it out of his sock, and he was glad that he was nearly home. Suddenly, nearby, a roe deer crashed out of the wood and bounded along the hedge. Halfway along the hedge it stopped and looked back, staring curiously in John's direction, unsure of what had disturbed it as it had browsed on the bramble leaves. John stood perfectly still and watched it a hundred yards distant as it inquisitively bobbed its head, and cautiously picked its delicate way closer. It stopped sometimes to test the wind and try to discern what the unfamiliar object was beside the fence. As it neared him John could see its large ears twitching and the velvety knobs of the growing antlers. Frightened to even blink he watched as the buck hesitated, and then came even closer until a sudden whiff of danger sent it bounding on its way with a dog-like bark to warn others of the imminent threat.

17

White House Shaw

John dared to move again so he set off across another field of winter wheat in the direction of White House Shaw, the last feed. He whistled as he threw the corn out along the track between the shaw and the dried up artichokes. As yet there were no catchers in place, but Reg had said they would soon have to make some up. John hurried, his foot squelched inside his boot, and he was wet. The rain had found its way down his neck, and he could feel it wetting his shirt. He was grateful that at last his feed bag was empty.

He had half filled it at the feed bin that stood near his pen, and again at a bin in the wilderness, but he found the extra weight had slowed him down on the wet ground, and had probably been the cause of his falling into the ditch.

He left the shaw and headed towards home, the walking made easier on the grass fields. He could see Reg's house and the caravan beyond the farm buildings. Some rooks flew up from their search among the cow-pats for food, and John knew that soon Reg would be waging war on them and their cousins, the crows and the jackdaws. The heifers out in the field came galloping over towards him, skidding to a halt and snorting and sniffing at the feed bag over his shoulder. He left behind him the peaceful woods and fields as he climbed the gate into the farmyard and stepped into the hubbub of the bustling farm.

THE FARM

The two tractor drivers were busy. One was scraping out the passages between the cubicles where the cows could lay down. The scraper at the back of the tractor collected the muck into a pile ready to be pushed into the large slurry lagoon. The other tractor was creeping slowly along beside the central manger pulling a large trailer that was churning silage down the chute and into the manger.

John walked past the din of the tractors and the cows and past a row of loose boxes. Suddenly a head appeared over the half-door of one as George the cowman stood up. He had been shaking out fresh straw, and his coat pocket was stuffed with string from the bales.

"Hello John, how are you getting on," he shouted across.

"O.K. thanks," John answered, walking across to the box.

"Time you've had a week of this weather you'll be wishing you was working in a factory," laughed George.

"Not me," John answered faintly, wondering if he might indeed be wishing that before long.

"Reg didn't look in a very good mood when I saw him earlier," George continued, "what you been doing to upset him?"

"Oh — I overlaid," John answered back and with a quick goodbye he hurried off through the farmyard. The big friesian bull in the bull pen lowered his great head threateningly as he went past, and John hoped that he would not be turned out with the heifers in a field that he might have to cross.

He walked quickly along the road that went past the farm manager's house, and turned off up the drive to the head keeper's house.

The slightly battered landrover stood outside the house which meant that Reg was in — John wondered what he should have done if Reg had been out. Perhaps he had better ask in case one day Reg was not back.

Reg shouted out of the kitchen window as he went past "I've got someone just called, so go and have a cup of coffee, and come back round when you're ready."

JOHN'S CARAVAN

Hanging his feed bag up in the shed, John realised just how wet and cold he now felt. The warmth of the caravan greeted him as he opened the door. The gas fire, which he had left turned down low, was sufficient to keep the caravan dry and cosy. He put the kettle on, and while it was boiling he changed his clothes, and spread the wet ones out on a chair to dry. He towelled his hair dry and turned on the radio while he drunk his coffee. The news reader informed him that it was eleven thirty, and he couldn't believe that the time had passed so quickly.

The caravan already began to feel like home and already it was starting to get as untidy as his bedroom had usually been; he found it a relief not to have his mum continually nagging about the mess. He put the empty mug in the sink along with the mug and bowl from breakfast. The washing up could wait. Reg appeared at his kitchen door as John walked across towards the house.

"Come on lad — we'll get some corn bagged up, then we can fill the bins up in the wood after dinner — that ought to be the last time they need filling."

They drove down the drive and along the road to the farm and pulled up in front of an old stable beside the granary. Inside was a pile of wheat, from which scuttled three mice as they opened the door.

"Go and get some of those empty plastic bags from over there beside the barn," Reg told him pointing in the direction of a barn that was half-filled with straw. John found the pile and returned with an armful of bags.

"You hold the bags open and I'll shovel the corn in," Reg instructed him as he picked up a large shiny shovel.

When eight bags were filled and stood by the door Reg straightened his back and suggested to John that he take a turn.

"How many bags do you need," enquired John diffidently after a few minutes — his back and arms were aching and there was still an awful lot of wheat in the pile.

"About twenty should do," Reg answered much to John's relief.

When the twenty bags were stood by the door, Reg backed the landrover up as close as he could get and they loaded in as many as there was room for.

Dinner

Dinner was ready when they got back to the house. Mrs. Plummer bustled round dishing up the delicious smelling food, while John washed his hands and then sat uncomfortably on a chair. He still felt a little out of place in the house even though Reg and his wife accepted his presence as they would have their own son. He still had not overcome his natural shyness.

"Come on John — you sit over there. I hope you like steak and kidney pud," Mrs. Plummer told him as she set down a plate piled high with pud, carrots, sprouts and mashed potatoes coated with thick brown gravy.

"Yes, I do, there's not much I don't like," John answered settling himself into the chair, and just remembering his manners in time, he waited for Mrs. Plummer to join them. He ate ravenously, not realising how hungry he was. He cleared his plate and ate two helpings of apple pie before he felt full.

Mrs. Plummer handed him the newspaper and a cup of tea when he had finished, and Reg muttered something about cleaning the kennels out, before he settled himself in the old armchair beside the Rayburn, and was soon asleep.

John finished his tea and looked through the paper while Mrs. Plummer cleared away and washed up. Reg showed no signs of stirring, so he thought he had better get on with the kennels.

The Kennels

The dogs came out of their sleeping quarters barking as he approached, making John feel a trifle unsure. They had been friendly enough when they were let out and John had been introduced, but now without Reg they thought of him as an intruder. There were three kennels, one of which stood empty. In the first one was Jet, an old black labrador bitch; her muzzle was grey and her legs were stiff. Her eyes had the tinge of blue that came with failing eyesight. The next kennel was occupied by her two daughters. They were both yellow but easily distinguishable, Honey being cream coloured and Amber a sandy colour.

John spoke Jet's name as he picked up the shovel and went into the old bitch's kennel to clear up the muck and bits of straw. He fetched a bucket of water and a broom, and swept the concrete down and refilled her water bowl. Then he ventured in with Honey and Amber. They stopped barking when he opened the gate and came up to him wagging their tails and fussing around him. Amber screwed her lips up and grinned at him, but John knew enough about dogs to know that this was a greeting and not a warning, because it looked very similar to a snarl. The yellow bitches surprised him by going into their sleeping quarters when he told them. He finished cleaning down the concrete before he called them back out. He bent down and stroked them as they each jealously pushed their heads into his hands demanding his undivided attention; it was nice standing there stroking the dogs and dreaming of one day having a dog of his own, but Reg's voice soon called him back for work.

"Let's get this corn out — dogs weren't any trouble were they?" Reg asked, looking as though he had just woken up.

They got in the landrover and slithered and bumped their way along the tracks until they came to John's pen. Reg expertly steered the landrover through the ruts allowing it to slowly pull itself out without spinning the wheels too much, so that it could gain maximum grip. They backed up as near to the bin as they could get and emptied the bags into it. "That should see you through the spring," Reg said as they clambered back into the landrover.

The return journey was just as slippery and they only narrowly avoided getting stuck. When they reached the farm they loaded some more bags in and set off to fill two of the bins on Reg's beat; by the time they had finished the afternoon was fading into the darkness and there was no time to take any more bags of corn out.

"That'll do for today — you better have an early night and then perhaps you won't overlay in the morning," Reg told him when they arrived back at the house.

"All right", John answered, resentment in his voice at being treated as if he were still at school. "Goodnight," he muttered as he walked across to the caravan.

Evening

He turned the light on. It was cold, and the washing up was still piled in the sink. He lit the fire and turned on the T.V. and sat down to watch the end of children's programmes. He had looked forward to living on his own, away from the parental nagging about untidiness and going to bed, but already he was discovering some unforeseen drawbacks, like the washing up still being there, and the fire not on, and now he wanted his tea. The only way he was going to get some was to set to and get it himself — perhaps being independent wasn't quite all it was cracked up to be, he thought.

He stirred himself from the chair, put the kettle on, opened a tin of baked beans, and toasted some bread. The bread started to smoke while he was pouring the hot water onto the tea bag and the baked beans stuck to the pan, but his hunger overcame his dislike of burnt beans and black toast. His meal finished he tackled the washing up, and left it heaped on the draining board to dry. He sat down again in front of the televison, but there was nothing on to interest him. Picking up a book he thumbed through the pages. Already he was tiring of his own company. Perhaps a moped would be the answer, at least he would be able to go out sometimes, with the nearest town seven miles away and the bus service nearly non-existent, there was little chance of that without his own transport. The nine o'clock news came on the television, but John was having difficulty keeping his eyes open, and he decided that perhaps after all he should have an early night.

Another Day

John woke up early enough to cook himself some breakfast the next morning. When he opened the door to go out he felt the icy cold north east wind sting his face. The sky was grey, and the thought of working outside all day was uninviting. The pheasants and all the little birds were waiting for him in the woods as he went round feeding. The exercise had warmed him through, but he could still feel the wind sting his face, and when he washed the kennels out, while he was waiting for Reg to get back, his hands and feet soon felt numb with cold. The dogs had not barked at him this time when he approached the kennels which made him feel less like a stranger.

After dinner Reg and John loaded some wire netting, some string, and a bill-hook in the landrover and spent the afternoon making up some catchers alongside the artichokes at Whitehouse shaw. They cut straight hazel sticks and V-shaped hooks to peg the netting down. Reg showed John how to shape the netting and hold it in place with the sticks. He hung the pegs on the wire, and propped the catcher up on the sticks as the other catchers were propped up, enabling the pheasants to get used to them and feed freely underneath. Reg fashioned a tunnel over the entrance hole which prevented any birds inside finding their way out again and then he stepped back and watched as John made up the next one. Reg believed, as John was to soon find out, that the best way to learn how to do something was to do it yourself, and under Reg's guidance he soon had the catcher completed.

A Moped

That evening after tea he went round to the headkeeper's house to borrow the local paper. Mrs. Plummer asked him in and he was glad of the company. John sat down and scanned through the advertisements for motor cycles and mopeds until he found one for sale at a price he could afford. He knew it would be old or have something wrong with it, but he enjoyed tinkering with engines and hoped it would be nothing more than he would be capable of fixing himself. Reg told him to use their phone and ring about it, adding that if it sounded suitable he would take him round in the landrover to see it that evening. So it was that the evening was spent in the purchase of the moped. They loaded it into the back of the landrover and Reg even offered to help John if there was anything he could not fix.

Chores

The rest of the week was spent with the usual chores of feeding and various odd jobs, and in carefully checking the wire netting of the laying pen because it was Reg's intention to start on catching up the pheasants that they would need the following week. John's evenings were spent tinkering with the moped until at last it was 'in good running order' instead of 'in need of attention'.

CATCHING UP

Monday morning dawned grey, and a light drizzle misted the caravan windows. John was disappointed as he had been looking forward to catching up and thought it would probably be too wet. Reg had already told him that, apart from getting muddy, the birds would knock themselves about more and were difficult to handle if it were too wet. John was therefore surprised when Reg told him he would come with him to set the catchers in Home Copse, the Pen Wood and Smiths. The day before when he had fed, John had only put a few handfuls of wheat under each catcher, ensuring the pheasants would be hungry when they wanted to set the catchers.

John half filled his bag with corn and he and Reg set off across the sticky ploughed field. John found it difficult to match his pace to that of Reg's long strides and soon he was out of breath and unable to ask half the questions he wanted to ask.

They reached the edge of the wood and Reg told John to whistle as he normally did when he fed — his attempts sounded worse than usual; the more John thought about whistling in front of Reg the more feeble was the attempt, aggravated by his breathlessness. It was a relief when Reg, after laughing and passing a rude remark about the noise, suggested that he should be the one to whistle. John, although he felt self-conscious, could not help but laugh at himself because it had got so bad that he could not even get his mouth in the right position.

Preparations

Moving quickly and quietly, they put several handfuls of grain underneath the catchers and pegged them down securely. Reg sprinkled a few grains in front of the tunnel and fastened the openings at the top with three hazel sticks which could quickly and easily be removed.

They continued on their way setting the catchers in the Pen Wood and Smiths before they headed back towards home.

"Just in time to have a cup of tea and fetch some sacks and then we'll go round them," Reg told him.

It never ceased to surprise John how quickly the time passed when he was busy, already it was 10 o'clock. They drunk their tea and then set off again, corn in their bags, string in their pockets, and sacks over their arms.

Collecting

When they reached the first catcher Reg signalled to John to stay back a few yards. He stood and watched as the head keeper quickly pulled the sticks from the top of the catcher, reached in and expertly grabbed the birds and put them into the sack. In a few seconds the first three cocks and two hens were captured. Reg put four in one sack and securely tied it with string. He handed John the sack with the other bird in it and turned his attention back to resetting the catcher. He carefully removed any feathers and brushed the dirt out of the tunnel; he checked the pegs and replaced the sticks in the top before sprinkling more wheat inside and round the entrance.

They walked towards the other catchers, getting six hens and a cock out of the second one and disappointingly only one cock bird out of the last one. It amused John to see the sacks laid on the ground moving about, and one sack that contained the last cock bird travelled several yards before John retrieved it from a puddle. Even when he slung the sacks over his shoulder the birds still hopped about inside.

On reaching the Pen Wood they walked along the edge until they reached a track that came up from the farm; here they laid the sacks, spread out on the ground. They could then collect them in the landrover later.

Reg let John take the birds out of the next catchers, another ten hens and one cock. He watched trying to be patient as the boy fumbled about attempting to grab them; he held one by its tail only to find the feathers came out leaving him with them in his hand. Eventually Reg gave him a stern warning on the danger of grabbing the birds by one leg — whilst it was all right to treat a chicken so, on no account must pheasants be handled in that manner; their legs broke so easily, and the only thing a pheasant with a broken leg was fit for was dinner.

They carried the sacks back through the wood and laid them out with the others, then they headed up towards Smiths. Here they caught another eight hens and three cocks which Reg carried back to where they had left the others, while John continued round and finished feeding. Reg in the meantime fetched the landrover and collected the sacks so that by the time John got home they were spread out on the floor of the shed.

After a double helping of stew and dumplings John set off once again round the catchers, and was disappointed to find only five hens and two cocks, although he was surprised to find a squirrel in one and two jays in another. The latter he quite easily caught and killed, though not before one had clamped its beak on his finger and made it bleed; the squirrel however was rather more difficult. Not fancying putting his hand in to get hold of it, and not finding it very easy to hit with a stick he was quite relieved when it found its way out of the tunnel and ran off.

While John had been round the catchers Reg had rushed round and fed his beat. He wasn't surprised that John had not caught very many, as in his experience at Stonelands they never did seem to catch birds during the middle of the day.

When the light began to fade they set off once again round the catchers, and by the time they returned it was dark and another seventeen hens and eight cocks had been added to the score.

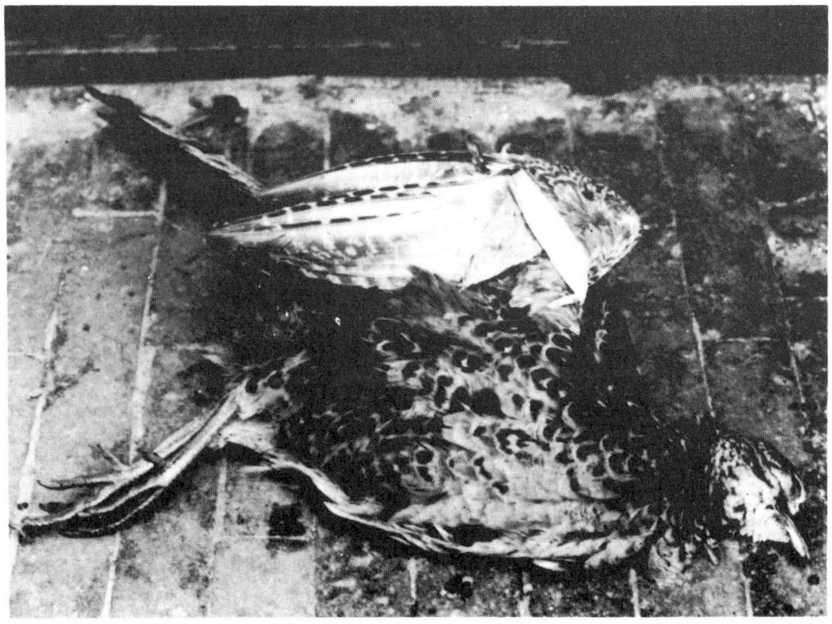

Figure 2.5   Brail in Position (inside)

As John prepared his tea he realised how tired he was; it was tiring carrying sacks of pheasants, and on working it out he had spent the most part of seven hours walking and his day's work wasn't finished yet. He would have even further to carry them when he caught the rest of his beat unless the ground dried up enough for Reg to take the landrover across the fields, which seemed very unlikely.

After he had eaten his meal he sat in the chair in front of the television with a second mug of tea, but half an hour later when Reg called round for him he was fast asleep. Reg thought it a shame to wake the boy, but getting the pheasants brailed was important, the sooner they were settled in the pen, the better

Brailing

John wasn't very keen to go outside again; whilst he found catching up interesting, he soon found getting the birds out of the sacks and holding them for Reg to brail was boring and cold. His feet were cold and his hands were scratched, but he tried to show continued interest as Reg deftly fastened the brails.

These were not the type that he had seen his uncle or old Tom using. They had been leather straps fastened with a paper fastener, whereas these

Figure 2.6 Brail in Position (outside)

were what Reg called ring brails, a circle of nylon tape that was slipped onto one wing, twisted and brought over the front of the wing with one or two flight feathers pulled through. It formed a figure of eight and kept the wing comfortably in the closed position preventing the birds from flying out of the laying pen.

When the last bird was safely put back in a sack, and these were well spread out over the floor, John was thankful that Reg asked him in for a bite of supper, and the mug of hot steaming cocoa soon warmed him through.

Further Catching

It was eight-thirty next morning before he set off once again round the catchers, allowing time for the birds to come off roost and find the corn. Reg had told him to spring the catchers — propping them up on the sticks, and to feed lightly up the feed ride; the following day he could catch the rest of his beat. It was nearly lunch-time before he struggled back home adding another dozen or so to the total.

The following week Reg started to catch his beat — one afternoon he took John with him and showed him how to set what he called 'drop' catchers. These were made from slats of wood made into a square about two feet across and about ten inches high, although some keepers used coops or hazel sticks. They were set by means of two hazel sticks balancing the catcher on a third long thin stick which was bent out from the back of it. Reg put some corn under the catcher and delicately set it up, then they both stepped back a few yards while an obliging cock pheasant completed the demonstration. Stepping on the thin looped stick to reach the corn, he released the other sticks and was safely trapped inside. Reg then removed him through a lid on the top — it was a good way of catching them but John could see it would be rather slow only catching one at a time.

By the end of February there were two hundred and fifty hens in the pen and thirty-five cocks, a new season had just begun. The keepers had cut fir branches and decked the pen with them, making clumps of cover for the hens to lay their eggs beneath. So now the pheasants had a month to settle down before the first egg would arrive at the beginning of April.

Figure 2.7   Winter in the Woods

The First
Snow
3

MARCH

Figure 3.1   The Snow-covered Landscape

THE FIRST SNOW

MONTH: **MARCH**

On the first day of March it snowed all day. John enjoyed going round feeding in the snow, and on his way back through the farm he could not resist the temptation to aim a snowball at Roger, the cowman's son, who also worked on the farm. He had begun to make friends with Roger and had been to the pictures with him the previous week, which had made a welcome change from staying in every night watching television. He caught Roger a treat as he went past on the tractor; he aimed the snowball in the back of the cab and Roger had turned round just as he threw it.

WILDLIFE IN THE SNOW

The pheasants in the laying pen looked different in the snow, they looked twice the size because they sat with their feathers fluffed up, and there looked twice as many in the pen, their camouflage colours were little use against the whiteness so that every bird showed. As soon as he neared the pen they all ran down to the farther most corners, still wild and unsettled yet. As he walked round throwing the corn out for them he was surprised at the flock of chaffinches and green finches that flew up in front of him and alighted again to scavenge for the grains of wheat amongst the pheasants, sitting in the bare trees at the end of the pen he could see doves and starlings waiting for him to depart so that they too could share in the feast.

It amused John to see the dogs romping about in the snow, Jet looked half her age as she bounded after the others and Honey kept rubbing her head and shoulder along the snow, then laying down and rolling, until her coat was plastered. On seeing John she careered towards him grabbing mouthfuls as she came and greeting him by jumping up and then shaking herself, showering him with dirty snow and water.

The snow ceased during the afternoon and the following morning John was fascinated when he fed round to see such a variety and quantity of footprints in the snow. Everywhere there were rabbit; even right out into the middle of one field, he saw the little round prints of a cat near the farm, the small prints of squirrels that ended abruptly at the foot of the trees. On his feed rides were numerous prints of birds, tiny little one of the robins, blackbirds and chaffinches that were waiting for him to feed, larger ones of pigeons that rose, wings clapping, as he neared the woods, even larger ones of the pheasants and of the odd moorhen he had noticed in the Wilderness. He noticed too the prints of foxes, like those of a small dog. So far as he could see it appeared that two had met and romped together in the snow. Perhaps they were like the dogs and enjoyed a game or perhaps one had intruded into the other's territory. His imagination worked overtime that morning, trying to piece together the nocturnal activities of the wildlife, busy that night as he had slept. Their secrets were half told when snow lay on the ground, their private lives not quite so private.

Figure 3.2   A Fox Snare in Position

SNARES AND TRAPS

Reg had promised John that he would, as soon as the birds were caught up, show him how to set some snares and traps. On seeing what was about John was getting impatient to get on with it. Now was the time to wage war on the vermin, before it had time to reproduce. The pheasants, both wild and released, would need all the protection they could get. In some areas, particularly East Anglia, where there was a conscientious keeper, good bags could be had from wild birds, but here in Sussex the keeper had to rely heavily on reared birds, and any wild ones were an added bonus. Even so, vermin control was very important and anything disposed of now would be no bother to them in the summer.

The snow was soon gone, a fine drizzle the following day disposed of it, and everywhere was left wet and dirty in contrast to the clinical appearance of the recent whiteness. A strong blustery wind and the sun soon worked together and dried the ground so that a day or two later Reg set off with John to set some snares and make some tunnels. They were walking along the track into the Pen Wood, when suddenly Reg motioned to John to stop. He too caught a glimpse of the stoat playing round an old rotten tree stump, he watched fascinated as Reg put his hand to his mouth and made a squealing sound, like that of a terrified rabbit. The stoat stopped and peered out from the root of the tree, they both stood still as Reg continued squeaking, their eyes followed the movements of the stoat as it darted from one bit of cover to the next, stopping to listen and then making its way still closer, unaware of the humans and curious at the noise. It had got to within three yards of them before realising its mistake and quickly retreating to the old stump.

"Wish I'd brought my gun", said Reg. "It'll be a good place to make a tunnel along that bank over there anyway. You might pick him up in a trap."

And so they set to work building a tunnel, until they had a natural looking mound, with room enough for the Fenn trap inside. The tunnel itself was barred with sticks across the entrances preventing access by larger animals

Figure 3.3   Tunnel with Fenn Trap Inside

and birds, allowing only for the passage of rats, stoats, weasels, squirrels and the like.

Reg then set to work showing John how to make a snare up, first cutting some hazel, and making it into what he called teelers. These were lengths about a foot long and sharpened at one end; the other end was pointed to a V shape and slightly split across the ridge. The snare itself was then wedged into this split leaving a loop as big as a man's head. They made up a few and then set off along the track until Reg spotted a likely place. He stuck the teeler in the ground, so that the loop was as high as the width of his hand off the ground and filled the gap, the other end of the snare he fastened securely to a fence post. As they walked on he explained to John what sort of places to look for and warned him about avoiding places which deer used. He knew from experience that roe deer would squeeze themselves under a fence, no higher than a foot from the ground and told John that sometimes he rested a stick across a few inches above the snare if he thought deer might use the site he had chosen. In his opinion this did not deter a fox from using it and prevented the deer from continually knocking the snare up or getting in it.

Darkness soon came down, once again the time had passed quickly. John was disappointed they had got no more snares set but he brightened up when Reg told him to set a few each morning as he went round, not too many at a time though else he would forget where he had put them and he must check them every day.

Figure 3.4   Fenn Trap in Set Position

John worked hard for the next couple of weeks, so that eventually he had sixty snares set and had built six tunnels. He found it added interest to his morning round; he had caught a rabbit and a cock pheasant in his snares but no fox although he knew there was one about because some mornings he could smell where it had been. "It's just a matter of time, be patient," Reg kept telling him. He had caught several squirrels in his traps — they seemed to be easy. He also caught a hedgehog and a couple of rats but not the stoat they had seen. He took the old 410 shotgun, that his uncle had given him, with him each morning too and had shot several more squirrels besides two magpies and a crow — indeed Reg and he were doing everything they could to destroy the winged vermin because, apart from the fox, they were perhaps the biggest threat to the wild pheasants.

PREPARATIONS

The clocks were altered towards the end of the month, and with the longer daylight in the evenings it really seemed as if winter were past, even the sun shone with some warmth and the leaf buds began to burst and the birds began to sing again.

Most afternoons saw the man and the boy preparing the release pens for the poults later in the year. The netting had to be pegged down again and checked for broken strands which would enable the poults to escape before they had had time to acclimatise to their new surroundings. Rotten posts needed replacing and one pen they extended — almost doubling its size. First they had rammed the eight feet high posts well into the ground then a single strand of thick plain wire was stretched tight along the top of them. The wire netting was then rolled out, stapled to the posts and fastened along the top of the wire. Reg allowed six inches spare at the bottom so that when it was turned outwards nothing could dig under the wire. They then strained a strand of barbed wire tight around the netting at ground level, a few pegs were cut and hammered into place to ensure it was held close against the ground and then they set about making the gates. The final job was to put up an electric fence all round, this was a strand of plain wire stapled to short posts with insulated staples, placed a few inches out from the pen and a few inches high, the electric fence unit could then be attatched when needed and any animal trying to dig in under the wire netting would be in for a nasty shock. Reg told John he was a great believer in the electric fence, it seemed a sensible precaution.

THE INCUBATOR

John spent one interesting afternoon watching the man who had come to service the Western incubator. Although he could not help much he soon

Figure 3.5   Western Incubator filled with Eggs

realised what a complicated business hatching pheasant eggs was. The whole mechanism in the machine was checked and greased where necessary to ensure that the machine ran smoothly and efficiently all the summer, keeping the eggs at exactly the right temperature, keeping them turned regularly, thus providing them with the best possible conditions in which to hatch.

Inside the machine were rows of trays held in place with clips that had been painted, some in red, some white and the rest in blue. Reg explained that he set the eggs usually on a Friday, filling up one third of the total number of trays; this he did each week until it was filled with the three different colours so that he knew which eggs were which. The eggs stayed in that machine for twenty one days when they were taken out and transferred to smaller hatchers for the last few days; his were Iron Clads, although there were several different makes in use. While in the Western the eggs were kept at a constant 99.7⁰ F, turned at frequent intervals automatically and a giant paddle forced the air round the eggs, the Iron Clads, however, were still air machines, working purely on convection for the air changes, with water in troughs inside that provided the necessary humidity for the eggs to hatch.

Listening to Reg and the engineer talking about the complications that some keepers encountered and the disasters that had occurred, John wondered that the eggs ever hatched. There was such a fine balance in obtaining the necessary requirements plus, they both agreed, a certain experience and touch were needed. Different conditions, for instance, needed different amounts of water put in the pans in the Westerns to get the ideal humidity and it was more a matter of trial and error over the years than reading it in an instruction manual.

IMPROVING WEATHER

March had come in like a lion but staying true to the old proverb it went out like a lamb. Primroses and violets were coming into flower, the fields were green with the growth of the corn and the yellow and green of spring replaced the drabness of winter.

Figure 3.6   Weasels with a Bird Victim

The Laying
Season
4

APRIL

Figure 4.1   The Poacher Fox

THE LAYING SEASON

MONTH: **APRIL**

For the last few days, when he had fed the pheasants in the laying pen, which were now fed entirely on pellets instead of wheat, John had spent some time searching for the first egg. He was determined that he should find it and Reg had laughed at the lad's enthusiasm, while appreciating the boy's keeness he couldn't resist playing a joke on him. John had just returned from his round of snares when Reg called him indoors for a cup of coffee; as they sat at the table Reg produced a pheasant egg from his pocket.

"All the time you've spent looking — I'd have thought you would have been the one to find this," he told the boy, somehow managing to keep a straight face, although he had to turn away when he saw the look of disappointment on John's face. Not until John held the egg did he notice it was a wooden dummy egg, nor had he realised that it was April Fool's Day until Reg laughingly reminded him. From then on the pheasant's gradually came on to lay, a few more every day.

April fifth was John's seventeenth birthday; he got up early and went off round his beat. He had all but stopped feeding the pheasants left in the wild. Some spring corn had been drilled and with the new growth they would fend for themselves.

ENCOUNTER WITH A FOX

He followed his daily route round his traps and wires; he had got nearly half way round when farther up the hedge he spotted something brown jumping about, at first from a distance he thought he must have caught a hare but drawing nearer he could see it was a fox. Aiming at the fox's head he pulled the trigger of the 410; it dropped to the ground blood gushing out of its ear, twitching as it died. It had made quite a mess of the hedge and it was well tangled up so it took John several minutes to unwind the snare which was twisted round the sticks, and to block up the hole in the hedge.

Figure 4.2   The Villain is Dead

Laid out on the grass the appeal that a fox held for some people was very apparent. His coat shone sandy red in the sun, the colour changing to black down his legs and the tip of his tail was white. His fur was soft and bushy, the beauty hiding the evil from many people's eyes. John had never actually touched a fox before; he had seen them shot and seen them hunted, but never had he touched one, again he looked over it, at the sharp white teeth, black shiny nose and the cat like feet. He would just have to take it home; Reg might not believe him otherwise. Although it was not very heavy held by its back legs it was surprisingly long, so it was with aching arms that John returned home sometime later.

Reg had seen him go past the window and put something in the shed and noticed the self satisfied look on the boy's face. He wondered what had caused the pleasure and he soon found out when John walked in.

"I don't think much of that new aftershave you're using this morning", he teased John, and not wanting to spoil the boy's pleasure he listened patiently to every detail, even going so far as to leave his breakfast to go and have a look at the fox.

"Go and have your breakfast then come back; my wife wants to see you" he said dismissing John, wishing to finish his breakfast in peace.

All the time he prepared and ate his breakfast John worried what he could have done to upset Mrs. Plummer . . . nothing he could think of.

A PLEASANT SURPRISE

When he entered the kitchen Reg pointed to some envelopes and a couple of parcels on the cupboard, it wasn't until he saw them that he remembered his birthday — he had quite forgotten with the excitement of his first fox. Opening the cards he felt a tinge of home sickness. This was his first birthday away from home and, although he had not really missed his parents and brothers up until then, the cards and presents aroused the latent feelings.

Reg interrupted his thoughts: "The weekend after next is Easter, I thought you might like a trip home then, there won't be much chance later on because we'll soon be getting busy. I'll look at your wires and traps for you."

"Thanks", answered John, "I should like to see my folks — it seems a long time since I last saw them".

John finished opening his mail, there was some money, a shirt and a lovely tie with pheasants on it from his Mum and Dad, and a sheath knife from his brothers. Inside the second parcel was some writing paper and a pen from his grandparents, making him wonder if they were dropping a hint of some kind.

Mrs. Plummer entered the room, "Good — I wanted to see you. Do you want a cup of coffee?" she asked, already putting a spoonful of coffee in a mug. John waited apprehensively for what she had to say next. She came over and sat at the table beside him, handing him the mug and the biscuit tin.

Discussing a Dog

At last she spoke; "Reg thought it was about time you got yourself a dog. My friend Mrs. Green has got two pups left to sell, they are black labradors, nothing fancy mind but from good working stock, so we thought we'd give you a bit towards the cost of buying one if you were interested."

Was he interested! Often he had thought about getting a dog, but he hadn't liked to ask. "I'd love one, but where could I keep it?" he asked.

"You can use the kennel that's empty next to mine — you'll have to look after the pup yourself and you will have to train it properly — I can't abide useless dogs," Reg butted in.

He laughed as the boy continued with more questions. "What colour were its parents, would he be able to have a bitch which he would prefer, how old were the pups and when could he see them?" he asked.

Mrs. Plummer attempted to answer his questions one at a time. Both parents were black, in fact the sire belonged to Fred, the neighbouring head keeper with whom Reg was quite friendly. There was one dog and one bitch left and she had already told Mrs. Green that they would prefer a bitch as Reg had got bitches. They were seven weeks old and she had arranged to take John to see them that afternoon, having been certain that John would be keen to have one.

"I think Mrs. Green had better keep it, if she will, until after Easter; there's not much point you getting it and then going off on holiday," she added.

John whistled as he completed the morning's work. He fed the hens, cleared out the water troughs and refilled them. He washed out the kennels, wondering while he did so what Amber and Honey would think of a pup in the next kennel.

Mrs. Plummer was amused at the speed John ate his dinner and was even more amused when he offered to dry the dishes after. "It's no good you rushing, I told Mrs. Green we'd arrive at half past two and I don't intend getting there any earlier," she told him good humouredly.

To John it seemed like an age while Mrs. Plummer tidied the kitchen and then herself, until at last she put her coat on and announced her readiness. All the while John had been trying to decide what to call the pup, names tumbling through his mind until he gave up. He thought of the dogs that he knew with inapproriate names. There was a thick-set yellow labrador called Nip and another black one called Prince which was by far the weediest looking labrador he had ever seen. It was a shame that naming a dog could not be left until it was grown up, then a name could be chosen to suit both its looks and temperament.

Suddenly Mrs. Plummer's voice broke into his thoughts: "I'm not taking you out in those dirty old clothes — you'd better go and tidy yourself up." The thought of getting changed had not occurred to John; embarrassed he quickly went off to do as he was told. He was back out by the time Mrs. Plummer had got the car out of the garage and he carefully shut the gate as she drove out. Reg insisted that the gate be kept closed at all times, ever since the previous year when the whole herd of cows had found their way into his garden and ravaged the entire vegetable plot and left great deep hoof prints all over the lawn.

At last they set off round the winding lanes. "Thought up any names yet?" enquired Mrs. Plummer.

"Not really", he answered, "although I quite like Sally."

"That's a nice name, you don't want one that sounds too much like the other dogs names and you don't want to choose one that you mind having to shout out — I think Sally is a very good name," she said.

They stopped in front of a beautiful olde worlde cottage, white painted with black beams and the garden full of flowers. As they went in the gate two black labrador bitches came over to greet them, barking but both wagging their tails. One of these John could see was the mother of the pups and she looked a lovely dog. Mrs. Green came out of the house, a plump elderly

Figure 4.3   A Labrador Puppy

woman wearing slacks and an old jumper. The two friends greeted each other and Mrs. Plummer introduced John, who by now was feeling very self conscious.

"Come on John, I expect you want to see the pups, there's two yellow ones and two black ones — one of the yellows is sold and the other we're keeping so that just leaves the two black. Mrs. Plummer said you'd want a bitch so I'm afraid that doesn't leave much choice," she said kindly.

They walked round the back of the house and over to a loose box which was part of a range of outbuildings. She opened the door and out tumbled four fat floppy puppies. They were gorgeous, the yellow ones straight away attracting John's attention. The rich creamy colour of their coats enhanced the darkness of their eyes and noses so that they looked more attractive and larger than the black ones, but when John picked them up there was actually little difference in their size. Chaos reigned for a moment as the pups eager to make friends jumped up sinking their sharp claws and teeth into clothing and flesh. One found John's shoe laces of great interest and another had found a lump of coal which it proceeded to carry around.

Turning to Mrs. Plummer Mrs. Green said, "Come on indoors, Mary, and I'll put the kettle on, we can have some peace then — would you like a cup John?"

"Yes, please."

"Well, I'll give you a shout when it's ready — can you put the pups back in the stable and bolt the door before you come in. I hate to think what havoc they would reek if left out unsupervised – I wouldn't have a flower left I don't think," she said makng her way to the back door.

The two women went into the kitchen chatting, leaving John to enjoy the attentions of the pups. They watched from the window as he looked carefully at each one and particularly at the black bitch. On closer inspection they really were all quite different. The black dog did not have such a nice tail as the others — it was thinner and his bitch was a little bit timid, yet it was affectionate when he made a fuss of it. The yellow ones definitely seemed more boisterous and forthcoming and he decided that he preferred the one he was to have more than the others; that would have been the one he would have chosen.

"Tea's ready," came the shout across the yard, interrupting his thoughts. The next few minutes were fun, particularly for the two women looking out of the window, for as soon as John opened the door to put the third puppy in, the first two would come tumbling out again; in the end he gave up and lowered them gently over the top of the door. He wiped his shoes carefully when he went in and was glad to wash his hands, for they smelled of puppies.

"Well, do you want her?" enquired Mrs. Green.

"Yes please," he answered. "Will it be all right for you to keep her for a few more days."

"Yes, Mrs. Plummer explained to me, that will be quite all right, you can pay for her when you fetch her too." Mrs. Plummer has given me some money so if you bring twenty five pounds that will do."

"That'll be fine — I'll fetch her as soon as I get back — I'm not quite so sure I want to go now," said John.

"Don't be so impatient — your mum and dad will want to see you," laughed Mrs. Plummer.

He finished the tea and a slice of fruit cake and asked if he could go and see the pups again. He crept quietly out and peered over the door without disturbing them. There they were in a box, a tangle of black and yellow, flopped out in complete oblivion, a paw twitching now and then, until one disturbed the mass by a long slow yawn and a stretch, it instantly sensed his presence and in a second they rolled out and waddled over to the door.

"Come on John — it's about time we were going — Reg will wonder where we've got to," called Mrs. Plummer.

The journey home seemed to take a fraction of the time that going had taken and Mrs. Plummer hardly had a chance to speak, John was so full of the puppies.

Reg opened the gate for them as they pulled into the drive, being unable to resist a comment on the length of time it took to look at one small puppy.

John went straight away to get changed back into his work clothes; he had arranged to go to the pub with Roger that evening and if he didn't hurry he would not have time to have some tea as well as feeding the hens and looking round for the eggs. Looking all through the fir boughs took some time and was somewhat disheartening when the birds were laying so few eggs, but each evening he had found a few more than the day before.

Getting ready for bed that night he thought over the day's events. He had enjoyed the evening out because he had met some more of Roger's friends who were all of much the same age as himself and were all used to a rural way of life. He had enjoyed the rest of the day as well and went to sleep thinking of Sally and her brothers and sisters.

The morning before Easter, John was up early and checked round his wires; he wanted to go home and see his family again but at the same time he was loathe to miss his daily round. Reg, he knew would keep an eye on things, but he hoped a fox would not get caught that weekend. He finished his chores after breakfast and packed a hold-all. Mrs. Plummer was going to take him to the station soon after lunch but it would be tea time before he was home.

John arrived back at the station after lunch on the following Tuesday, he rang through to Mrs. Plummer and a quarter of an hour later Reg pulled up in the landrover. "Did you have a nice time?" he asked, quickly adding "what have you got in that big parcel?".

John laughed, "Mum sent me back with a food parcel — I told her you looked after me well enough but she still insisted. In it there is a tin of biscuits, a chocolate cake, some chocolate biscuits and an apple pie – oh! I nearly forgot there's I don't know how many bars of chocolate."

"Were they glad to see you?".

Yes, especially my brothers. They thought I'd grown, so I told them that was proof I was being well looked after. I told them all about the puppy, they thought Sally was a nice name and my brothers wanted to see her. Would it be all right if they came over for the day sometime, they'd love to see where I am and to meet you and Mrs. Plummer?".

"Of course they can come, you ought to tell them to leave it until June though — then there'll be all the chicks for them to see as well."

"That's a good idea — I'll write and tell them. I'm glad to be back though — I missed my beat — you didn't catch a fox did you?".

"Yes," Reg answered, disguising a smile at the look on John's face — adding, "It wasn't in one of your wires though — it was in one of mine."

John was soon changed into his work clothes and looking for Reg. Although he hadn't told him to get on with anything Reg was pleased to see the lad interested in what had been going on while he was away. "Mrs. Plummer will take you over to pick up the pup tomorrow afternoon — that is if you still want it," said Reg as they searched round the pen for eggs.

"Of course I do — that'll be great if I could get her tomorrow."

PREPARING A KENNEL

When he had finished work and ate his tea he set about scrubbing out the empty kennel with disinfectant and washing out the run. He oiled the hinges on the door and the gate and when he put the oil back in the shed he sorted through a box full of old dishes and troughs, eventually settling for an old enamel dish for a feed bowl and an old churn lid for water.

The following evening Sally was installed in the kennel, she looked small and pathetic sitting by the gate in such a large kennel. John had given her a good bed of wheatstraw and at Reg's suggestion had bought some biscuit meal from Mrs. Green so that he could slowly change her over to the food that Reg used for his dogs. Honey and Amber had greeted the pup with some suspicion at first, but Sally had laid down on her back and let them sniff her through the wire and they soon lost interest. Jet looked bored with the whole proceedings having seen it all before. John mixed a little tinned meat in with a measure of biscuit and dampened it with warm water, she had eaten it greedily, but now, as John was in the caravan making himself a cup of tea, she sat by the gate and yapped. The barks intercepted with a howl now and then. John ignored the noise for half an hour before deciding that perhaps he had better seek expert advice.

"What shall I do to stop her barking?", he asked when Reg answered the bang on the kitchen door.

"Leave her for a bit longer, if she hasn't stopped I should give her a stern talking to and if she still doesn't shut up roll up a newspaper and hit her — not too hard though."

So John returned to the caravan and warmed her a little milk, which he gave her at the same time pleading with her to be quiet. He heard her yap a few more times, but then she was so quiet that he began to worry whether she was all right. Just before he went to bed he crept out to see and she was curled up fast asleep in the straw.

The next morning he could not resist playing with her when he fed her. Consequently he was late getting back from his rounds. By the time he had eaten his breakfast Reg had gone. Mrs. Plummer answered the door and explained that Reg had to see Mr. Brinklow and what he wanted John to get on with. She also hinted that perhaps it would be better in future if John played with Sally after he had finished work and not before he started!

THE SEASON PROGRESSES

By the middle of April the hens were laying quite a few eggs each day and if it had rained they were very muddy so John had the job of washing them most evenings. The days were getting longer and so were the hours of work. The cuckoo had arrived and every evening the woodcock flew low over the

Figure 4.4   Pheasant Eggs Laid under Fir Boughs in Laying Pen

trees, their peculiar call of grunts and squeaks could be heard in the dusk marking out their territories — Reg said the proper name was 'roding'. John liked the woodcock, he found them interesting birds, completely camouflaged on the ground until they suddenly rose in zig zag flight through the trees. They had short legs and long beaks and black beady eyes. He had found a part grown chick in the wood a few days before and now watched out for any more, not knowing whether to believe the story that a woodcock would carry its young when disturbed. He hoped to be able to voice his own opinion when next the subject was raised.

AN EARTH IS FOUND

One afternoon later in the month Reg and John had a look round the fox earths on the estate and found one was occupied. There were four main entrances to this particular earth and there were well worn tracks between the holes. The bluebells on the bank below were flattened where the cubs had played and, laid untidily around, were the remains of rabbit, pheasant and a roe deer kid. John expressed his surprise at a fox taking a fawn, but Reg explained that a roe would frequently have twins and occassionally triplets so that when they were new born the doe would have difficulty in warding off a hungry fox and guarding both fawns from its attentions.

Quickly they returned home to collect the spades and gas to deal with the earth, but just as they were leaving Fred pulled up in his pick-up. They explained hastily what was up and Fred suggested that he should come along and bring his terrier that John had not noticed curled up on the seat beside him.

The three of them sqeezed into the front of the landrover. The black and tan terrier sat on Fred's lap quivering with excitement, his paws on the dashboard and his scarred nose pressed up against the window.

They left the landrover and walked up through the wood to the earth. Reg carried his gun and a spade, John next with another spade, a spoon tied on the end of a long stick and a tin of Cymag. Fred followed with the terrier whimpering and squirming in his arms. They stood back from the holes a little way up the bank, Fred set the terrier down and they watched in silence as the little dog inspected all the holes before deciding which one to enter. Fred and John laid down on the ground between the holes and listened to the noises beneath, Reg stood alert and ready with the gun. The subterranean noises continued for several minutes when suddenly a shot rang out and then another. John had not seen the vixen bolt, but there she was laying in the bluebells her muscles quivering in the spasms of death. The terrier was still yapping deep in the ground, listening with his ear to the ground the barking sounded very distant, but listening at a hole it sounded

Figure 4.5   Remains of Pheasants and Rabbits Round the Entrance of a Fox Earth

Figure 4.6   The Plucky Terrier

quite near. Fred and Reg started to dig above where they estimated the dog to be situated, but even as they dug the terrier pushed the cubs farther back up the tunnel so that they had to start again a yard or so farther back. They knew from experience when they were nearing the terrier and dug carefully until suddenly they broke into the tunnel and a short black tail appeared. A small cloud of steam arose round the terrier as he backed out of the newly dug hole, his face was coated in earth and blood and his muddy tongue was hanging out as he gasped the fresh air but with a quick look at Fred he resumed his pursuit. Fred knelt down and pulled his dog back out by his tail, and it was found that this time he held tight onto a dead chocolate brown cub.

"Here lad, hold onto him while we dig the rest out," shouted Fred.

John found it extremely difficult to hold the squirming creature, who had no other thought in his head than to finish off the rest of the cubs — a job that Reg and Fred had soon accomplished. There were five altogether, three dogs and two vixens, perfect miniatures of the adults except for their thick fluffy chocolate brown fur which only changed to chestnut as they grew older.

"That's a good day's work, better off without them in the middle of the shoot," said Reg as they loaded themselves back in the landrover. "Has the vixen chopped the terrier much?" he added.

"No, its nothing much — he'll soon be as right as rain," answered Fred peering at the terrier who was now sitting quietly on his lap. There was still earth and blood all over his face and his gums and teeth were caked with mud. "My other terrier got badly bitten last week — I think she has lost the sight of one eye and she's a couple of teeth missing" he continued. "She still thought she should come today — they never give up do they?".

"You'll stop for a cup of tea," enquired Reg. "By the way did you call for anything special I never gave you time to hardly say hello?".

"Yes, I was wondering if it was o.k. for me to have some wood shavings again this year for the brooder huts — I know you usually have plenty on the farm but I thought I'd better ask," answered Fred.

"That'll be all right," said Reg as they pulled up in front of his house, "they've just had a load in on the farm and I'll see the manager — you can help yourself then — they're in the usual place."

Turning to John he told him to put the gear back in the shed and then come for a cup of tea.

By the end of April spring was in full bloom, some of the woods were carpeted with bluebells and the air was filled with their scent. Reg and John continued in their pursuit of vermin, visiting the fox earths they knew of regularly; they found and gassed another litter and accounted for three adult foxes. The weather had turned wet and instead of being able to get on with assembling the equipment on the rearing field, Reg was trying to find some indoor work to get on with. He was impatient to get the equipment out because he had already put some eggs in the incubator and he knew even when it left off raining it would be a day or two before the ground dried sufficiently to take a tractor and trailer over it without leaving ruts.

TRAYING THE EGGS

John had watched Reg traying up the eggs and marvelled at the gentleness with which Reg's large rough hands placed the eggs carefully in the trays, straight rows across the trays and with the pointed ends downwards. He then pushed cottonwool in the gaps along the edges of the trays so that the eggs were kept firmly packed. When Reg had put the trays in the Western incubator John had watched as they turned. He soon realised why Reg had been so thorough with the way he had trayed the eggs as they seemed to be tilted at an alarming angle and with the paddle whirring continuously if a tray slipped out it would cause a terrible mess.

The shed that housed the incubators was in view of the laying pen which proved useful when one day John spotted a crow fly out of the pen with an egg in its beak. From then on Reg made sure his old single barrelled 12 bore was within easy reach if either should see it again; once it had found an easy supply of food it would certainly be back and probably with its mate.

Figure 4.7   Getting the Eggs Ready

Reg had filled some of the trays for the first week's setting. There were not enough eggs to fill them all, but if he did not get the early eggs set they would soon get stale and also he would be unable to use some of his rearing equipment twice, which he needed to do to rear the five thousand chicks he required. John soon grew used to the hum of the incubator motor buzzing away in the corner of the shed and to handling the ever increasing number of eggs. Sometimes there would be a double yolker the size of a hen's egg and sometimes a soft shelled one which felt as though it were made of white rubber. When Reg had carefully trayed the eggs John was surprised at the variations in colour ranging from dark brown to pale blue and occasionally with white spots on. When it had been wet during the day the eggs were very muddy which meant that they needed washing every night. John too was soon hoping that the weather would change for it certainly made the work much pleasanter.

"Every year we get a bad spell of weather in April," Reg told him, "country folk call it the blackthorn winter as it usually coincides with the blackthorn flowering."

"Well I'll be glad when the sun shines again and the eggs won't need washing," John had answered.

(a) The Payne-Gallwey Coop. A cheap and simple style of coop.

(b) Rearing-Coop for Pheasants. The shutter is hinged, and serves also as shelter from sun and rain.

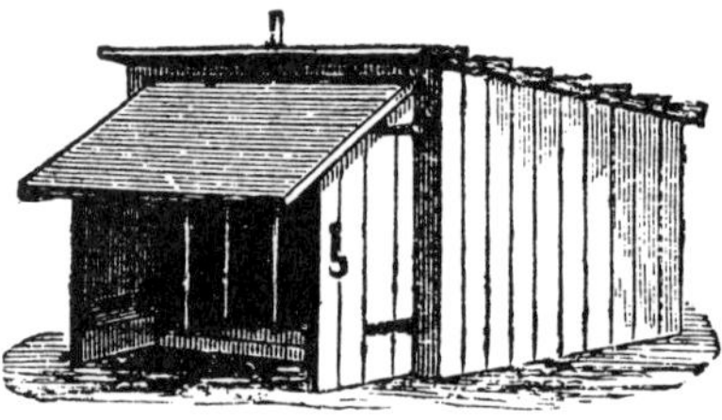

(c) Rearing-Coop with Sliding Double Roof. The sliding roof with folding shutters forms shelter from sun and rain.

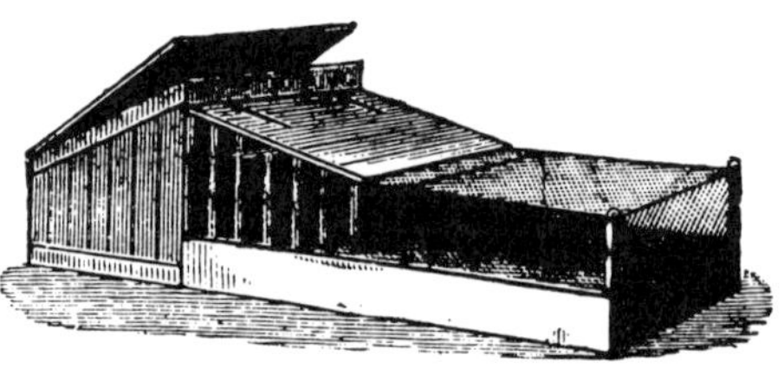

(d) Rearing-Coop and Run.

(e) Rearing-Coop with Cage-Run.

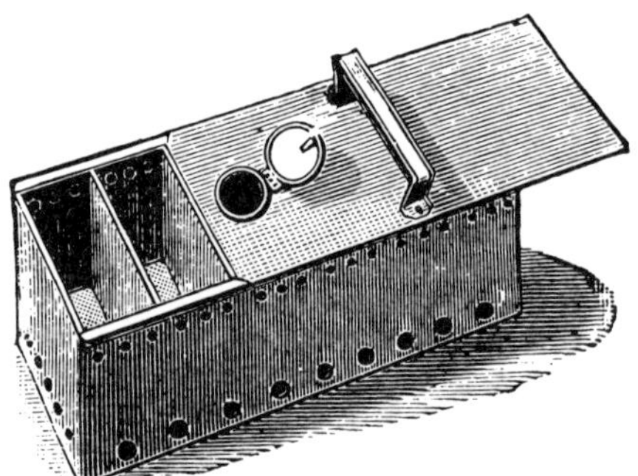

(f) Carrying-Box for Pheasant Chicks.

Figure 4.8   Various Types of Rearing Coop and Carrying Box (Based on old-style designs)

Rearing
Preparations
5

MAY

Figure 5.1   (Above) Early 1960s Row of sitting boxes and Broody Hens — The Old Style Incubators.
(Below) Early 1960s Releasing Young Poults Alongside a Wood.

REARING PREPARATIONS

MONTH:MAY

The month began cold and wet, but spring was flourishing. There was white blossom in the hedges and bluebells in the woods. The leaves were fresh and green and the cuckoo called incessantly. The hen pheasants in the pen were laying well and had nearly reached their peak. John grew tired of washing the eggs every night, but with practise he could handle them a lot quicker now, although occasionally one that was wet and slippery would slide through his fingers and crack as it hit the table.

SORTING THE EQUIPMENT

By the end of the first week of May the wet weather had given way to the sun and a warm drying wind enabling Reg and John to start assembling the huts and pen sections on the field next to Reg's house where they would rear the chicks.

Reg had arranged to borrow a trailer from the farm and hitched up behind the landrover they were soon ferrying the equipment from the tractor shed where it had been stored for the winter across to the rearing field. All the equipment had been dismantled the summer before when it had been finished with and meticulously stored away. The nets from the tops of the runs had been tied up above onto the rafters where the rats and mice would be unable to to reach them. John thought the different stacks of sections looked like some giant jig-saw puzzle, but Reg had been doing the puzzle for the last fifteen years so he was able to fit it all together with ease. Reg skilfully reversed the trailer along side the shed and they started to work.

"Come on John — take hold of the far side of that section and we'll put it on the trailer," said Reg pointing at one pile.

"Right – now one off that pile," he continued and going round again they soon had two complete huts loaded on the trailer. They tied a rope across the load and then carefully made their way out to the field.

Figure 5.2   Getting the Equipment Ready

John leaned on the trailer enjoying the warm sunshine and watching Reg as he paced out the field, marking with his heel where the first four huts were to be placed, leaving enough room to drive between the hedge and the front of the huts.

The Layout

The first section they lifted off was the floor which was placed with one corner on the first heel print, the next four sections they unloaded were the front, back and two sides which they laid in place around the floor, lastly the roof was lifted off and leaned against the hedge.

"Hop in lad and move the landrover up about twelve yards," Reg called to John as he checked the distance to the next hut.

Now John was used to his moped and had once driven a tractor, but the landrover was a bit different and he hadn't driven it before. After stalling it twice he managed what Reg laughingly called a kangaroo start, making the trailer jolt and the remaining sections rattle together.

"Now you're seventeen you ought to do something about having driving lessons — a keeper is little good these days if he's not got a licence and by the looks of it you've got quite a lot to learn," Reg added.

"I had been thinking about it," answered John.

They unloaded the rest of the sections and returned for another load. John was sent to fetch the bucket containing all the nuts and bolts which Reg could remember leaving under the table in the incubator shed. When he got back to the landrover Reg suggested John should collect the eggs while he took the trailer round as it was nearly dinner time.

While John searched through the fir boughs for the eggs his mind wandered to what a keeper's life involved; when he had applied for the job he had not realised half of what it did involve. Most people he thought probably considered the shooting season as the busiest time, but they were wrong. There seemed always to be some job that needed doing whenever there was an hour of daylight and John was already finding that there were a lot of daylight hours at this time of the year.

After dinner when they had off loaded the rest of the sections they started to assemble the first hut. The landrover tool kit was raided for a spanner to fit the nuts and a hammer was unearthed from the dirt under the seats to persuade reluctant bolts into place. By the end of the afternoon they had six huts assembled and lined up.

"That'll do for today, at least we've made a start — it must be tea time," said Reg as he walked over to unhitch the trailer. "We'll leave this here — I don't expect they'll need it on the farm, and if they do they know where it is."

MORE EGG COLLECTIONS

After his tea John went about collecting the eggs for the second time that day and he was annoyed to find five that had been eaten by the pheasants, only the shells remained. Up until then egg eating had not been a problem but five was too many. Reg had been carefully filling any eaten eggs he had found with a mixture of mustard and cayenne pepper and while it did not ever really stop them eating their eggs it did seem to deter them. Nevertheless, the hens had laid well and there were fewer eggs that needed washing. While the eggs were drying he went back to the pen and fed the birds with a bucketful of pellets, he stood and watched them as they came up to feed forming a thick line along the ground where he had thrown the food. The cock birds clucked quietly to the hens and they looked magnificent in the setting sunlight. Their plumage shone like burnished copper and the iridescence of their heads contrasted their red wattles. With tufted ears pricked they tip-toed around full of self importance.

John turned and went back to the incubator shed to tray the remaining eggs. He placed them pointed end down in the paper maché trays that Reg called keyes trays, each tray held thirty eggs and already there was quite a pile of filled trays waiting to be transferred to the incubator trays as soon as they came empty.

He checked the Western, the temperature was right and it was humming

Figure 5.3   A Hen Sitting

busily at one end of the shed, opposite were the Iron Clads which would soon be in use. He shut the door, his work done for the day but still there was Sally to tend to. He opened the kennel gate and she scampered out, her tail wagging furiously. John sat down in the grass and tried to fondle her ears, but she was more intent on finding something to chew at, she found a stick and laid down nearby, the stick held between her paws like a bone. Her coat shone and she was growing fast but John had made no attempt to train her yet. He rose and walked over to the caravan to fetch the puppy's supper– it was no trouble to get her back in the kennel when he had a bowl in his hand, but while he had been preparing it she had pulled the eider-down half off his bed and made off with one of his slippers.

The sun was long set before John was in the caravan and there was little time left to read or watch T.V.

The next morning John was looking round his snares and traps when he diverted his route to visit a fox earth he knew of in the Wilderness. The holes were in a bank and before he reached it he could see it was occupied. The earth was worn smooth and the entrances were littered with the remains of rabbits and pheasants. On his return John informed Reg of his discovery and half the morning was spent with gassing the earth. Reg handled the white powder with respect, pushing it well down the holes with a long handled spoon before filling the entrance up tightly with spades full of earth.

They then continued erecting the rearing equipment and by the end of the week they had all twenty huts spaced out in two straight lines across the field, the only other interruption to their work during the week was transferring of the eggs from the Western to the Iron Clads on the Thursday afternoon. John helped Reg pick up handfuls of the warm eggs and lay them on their sides on the trays out of two of the hatchers. While John had collected and washed the eggs that evening Reg had packed the eggs from the keyes tray into the emptied Western trays, ready to be put in next morning.

Whenever John or Reg was in the incubator shed they would check the temperatures of the machines and it was on the Sunday evening when John had a last look round after doing the eggs that he noticed a very wet ugly chick wobbling about on top of the eggs. The thermometers were hung slightly above the eggs on the tray, level with a glass window in the front of the Iron Clad, which necessitated the use of a torch to be able to read the temperature accurately. When John shone the torch a little lower onto the eggs, besides the wet chick he could see several of the eggs had minute cracks appearing about two-thirds of the way up from the pointed ends. He peered in through the window of the other machine but could only discern cracks in two of the eggs. He knew Reg would be in later, as he did last thing every night to look round so didn't think it necessary to tell him.

The next morning he was up early and he went quietly across to the shed and once again shone the torch through the glass. He was disappointed because he could see very little, the windows were steamed up with condensation, he could just see near the front one or two chicks, dark and wet, their heads wobbling in an effort to raise them and focus on the torchlight. When John had finished the eggs that evening and he shone the torch in he could see dry, fluffy chicks, their striped heads turned towards the light. The stronger ones, being drawn to the light through the window had dropped to the lower level and John could see them jumping up in an attempt to peck the condensation from the glass. He watched the chicks for a quarter of an hour, smiling as the stronger ones still on the top tray would move towards the torchlight as though drawn by a magnet, only to fall off the tray and join their stronger companions below. He smiled too at the total disregard they had for their brethren, treading on top of them as though they were not there.

"Oh John, there you are."

Reg's voice made him jump; he had been so absorbed watching the chicks that he hadn't heard Reg come in.

"When will you take them out?" asked John.

"Not till tomorrow afternoon, then we'll know how many we've got. I can never judge although you know if you've got a bad hatch because the windows don't steam up — fewer chicks less condensation. Humidity in the

Hatching Stage 1   Hatching Stage 2

Hatching Stage 3   Hatching Completed

Figure 5.4

Iron Clad is a vital factor for a good hatch; if it is too dry the membrane inside the eggs dries out and the chick is trapped inside." Reg continued.

USING GAS CYLINDERS

"Can you give me a hand, I've been ringing the firm all day because they never delivered the gas cylinders last week, and it turns out they left them up at the farm and I've only just found out. We must get two fixed up tonight as we'll need them tomorrow — you did fix the heaters up in the huts as I asked you this afternoon didn't you?"

"Yes", answered John, "I think they are about the right height, and I put some shavings in the first two huts."

"Good — come on then if you've finished, we'll go and get a couple of cylinders", said Reg, hunting through a box under the table for a large adjustable spanner.

They heaved two of the heavy red cylinders of propane gas into the landrover and rattled their way out to the rearing field. They manoeuvered them into position at the back of the first two huts and John watched as Reg tightened the regulator onto the cylinder and then pushed the pipe from the heater inside the hut firmly onto the regulator. He checked inside the hut and slightly lowered the chain on which the heater was hung. At Reg's request John turned the knob on the top of the cylinder and he could hear the hiss as the gas went through the regulator. Reg lit the heater and waited a moment until the gauze in it glowed red. They moved to the second hut and lit the other heater. Backing out of the hut Reg straightened up and turned towards John.

"Whatever you do lad, never, never try and light a heater if the hut smells of gas, there's more than one keeper landed up in hospital through doing just that. If the heater has gone out, always turn the gas off and drop the window or open the door for a minute or two before you light it again."

"Are you going to leave them alight tonight?" John asked noting the warning he had just received.

"No, I'll turn them off and light them again first thing in the morning. I don't know, every year we seem to get behind getting the rearing equipment up — I bet if I started in February something would still go wrong at the last minute. We'll get the night shelters put up tomorrow morning, at least being a small batch this week we only need two huts", answered Reg as they set off home in the landrover.

ERECTING NIGHT SHELTERS

The following morning after they had visited their snares and traps followed by breakfast, they loaded the trailer with night shelter sections.

These were wire netting sections with boards round the bottoms; struts were placed across the top of the four sections, joined with wire to form a square and these supported the green corrugated plastic sheets that bolted on to form the roof. They completed the shelters for the first six huts and while John collected the eggs Reg finished preparing the huts for the chicks. He placed a sheet of hardboard across the back of the hut so that it was wedged to form a curve — not only would this make the floor area smaller until the chicks grew stronger but it also blocked off the corners. He fetched four Keyes trays, four glass drinkers, a bucket full of chick crumbs and a bowl. He put two Keyes trays in each hut and spread a bowl full of crumbs out on each one and he smoothed the wood shavings level. The drinking fountains he left outside the doors to the huts. Reg went back to the shed and mixed some vitamin powder into a bucket of water and picking up four short lengths of hosepipe he returned to the rearing field. He filled the glass jars and put the base on top, quickly turning them over, the hosepipe he pushed in around the base so that it nearly filled it, leaving only a small amount of water available for the chicks, without this the tiny chicks would be likely to drown, even though the water was only an inch deep. For years he had used small stones round the bottom, but the hosepipe was much easier to take out and clean. The drinkers he left outside the huts ready.

MOVING THE CHICKS

After dinner Mrs. Plummer found the two cartons she had saved when she fetched her groceries, and having lined them with newspaper Reg and John returned to the incubator shed. Reg pulled an old table across under the door of the first Iron Clad and instructed John to be ready to catch any chicks that jumped or fell out. While he took the tray out, he brushed the good chicks off the tray with his hand so they fell over the back and then pulled it right out and put it on the table. He then methodically counted the chicks from the bottom of the machine into one of the cartons, his large rough hands delicately handling them. John knew better than to talk whilst Reg counted as he busied himself inspecting the trays of egg shells. There were several that had not hatched as well as a lot of empty shells. Somehow some of the shells had got packed inside others. Everywhere there were tiny pieces of shell where the chicks had chipped their way out. There were two eggs with the chicks still cheeping inside; they had pecked all the way round, but had not been able to lift the lid off. John could see their little beaks each with a minute hook on the tip that they used to pierce the shell. He lifted the lids off and instead of being wet the chicks had almost dried out. He placed them back on the tray and looked in the box, it was a seething mass of chicks, an odd one was black and a couple were black and white.

Figure 5.5   Egg Tray after Hatching

"There's over two hundred out of there, not bad at all", said Reg straightening his back.

"Did you notice those black and white ones?" asked John.

"Yes, they look like magpies — they'll not stay white though — as soon as they get their adult feathers they'll change to black, although occasionally one will have a few white feathers on it's throat", answered Reg.

"Why don't you like black ones?" asked John remembering that Reg had not wanted to put any black cock birds in the laying pen.

"They're a nuisance, you see nearly all the black ones have got white tips on their wings — well the other little blighters all peck and pull at them until they make them bleed, and very soon they've killed them off," Reg explained. "Now, can you take this box full out and put them in the first hut while I count them out of the other hatcher."

Placing Chicks in Rearing Huts

John carried the carton quickly out to the field, and opened the door of the hut. Inside it was warm and the wood shavings smelt sweet. He put the box down carefully and started placing the chicks under the heater. He had not quite finished when he saw Reg carrying the other box, coming towards him.

"Haven't you finished yet?" Reg called out.

"No — not quite, I'm afraid of hurting them" John replied.

"The easiest way is to very carefully tip them out, it only takes a second, then you can spread them out afterwards. Here, take ten out of this box and then the numbers will be even in the two huts", Reg told him.

John did as he was told and then carefully placed the drinkers inside the hut.

"What have you given them to drink — lemonade?", he asked as he walked over to Reg.

"No, it's an antibiotic and vitamin mixture — they have it for the first few days and it helps to give them a good start", Reg answered.

They stood and watched the chicks inside the hut, already some of them were pecking at the food and others were taking their first drink. The noise of their cheeping was ear piercing as they investigated their new surroundings.

"Come on lad — we'll go and sort those egg trays out, then we'll come back and check them, they won't take long to settle down."

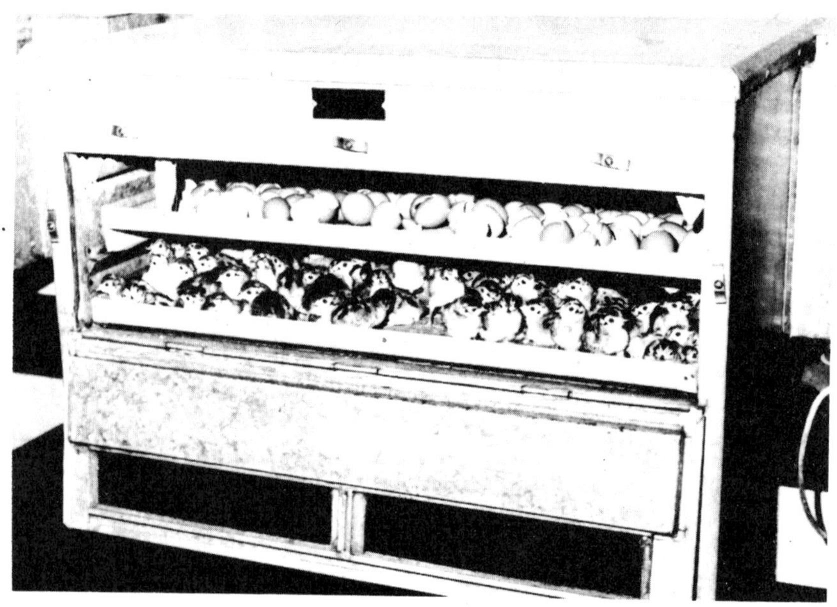

Figure 5.6   Chicks Ready to be Moved

CLEANLINESS IS ESSENTIAL

Reg turned the tap on to fill the tank outside the incubator shed that they used for washing up the equipment and then they both sorted through the two trays of egg shells and unhatched eggs. There were a few weak chicks that Reg killed by pressing their necks on the sides of the trays, then he opened up a few of the unhatched eggs with his penknife. Most of them were clear; these looked like fresh eggs and were infertile he explained to John; a few had dead chicks in and these had obviously died during hatching. Reg pulled one out of the shell to show John just how complicated it was for them to hatch. The chick had to be in the correct position. He also pointed out the unabsorbed egg yolk attached to the chick's navel below its vent.

Reg and John tipped the debris into a dustbin and John choked as the fluff from the chicks floated into the air as he tapped the tray to rid it of the particles of shell. Reg had forgotten about the tap running outside, but was soon reminded when they went to put the trays in the tank.

"Oh dear", he muttered, "bale a drop of water out while I measure the disinfectant."

John did as he was asked and waited for Reg to mix the disinfectant in before he submerged the trays.

"Come on — we'd better go and see if them chicks are all right", said Reg.

When they reached the huts Reg motioned John to look through the slightly open window with him.

"That lot are o.k. — see how they've settled down leaving a circle empty directly under the heater — that gives them a chance of a bit more heat if it turns colder."

Moving onto the second hut they peered through the window.

"They're a bit on the cold side — look they are huddling up in the middle — I'll lower the heater a couple of inches — that should do the trick", explained Reg.

"I think we've earned a cup of tea — I think Mary's gone out this afternoon so we won't get told off", continued Reg as they walked toward the kitchen door.

Half an hour later Reg went back to check the chicks again while John set about scrubbing the trays. Despite the soaking it took quite a lot of scrubbing to remove the gluey stuff which was the 'placenta' of the chicks. The tiny specks of shell were difficult to get rid of too although the dark green slimy droppings came off quite easily after the soaking.

Reg returned and asked John to wipe out the insides of the hatchers with disinfectant and to burn the dirty hessian which had covered the bottom tray. Reg swept the floor and swilled it down and then they collected and washed the eggs.

EVENING REFLECTIONS

His tea that evening had a distinct flavour of disinfectant — no matter how many times John washed his hands the smell remained. Later when he was getting ready for bed he saw Reg leave the house with a torch in his hand and walk across the field to the huts — checking that all was well before he went to bed.

When Reg had finished his tea, he had sat in the old armchair beside the Rayburn, lit his pipe and thought of seasons past. Every year he felt a thrill at the sight of the first chick — every year it held the same magic for him. His thoughts turned to John — just embarking on his career. Up until then the lad had worked willingly and had not minded the long hours and little time off, but now was the start of the testing time; even longer hours and repetitive work aggravated sometimes by the weather. He had grown used to the hard slog through the summer months knowing it would soon pass, but for John he knew the work would seem endless and while his friends would be enjoying trips out and holidays he would be tied to his pheasants. **Keepering was much more a way of life than a job.** Reg's thoughts progressed to his wife, Mary. She was not interested in keepering but she had adapted herself to his lifestyle and seemed reasonably content, although if she had not passed her driving test several years ago she might

Figure 5.7   Chicks at Three Days Old on Grass

not have been so content when their children had left home. It was a lonely life for her with him working all hours through the summer and out most winter nights patrolling around the estate; indeed, he considered himself a lucky man, enjoying his work and married to a woman who could put up with it.

Reg got up from the chair and walked over to the window, he looked out and saw John playing with Sally — he had certainly been conscientious in his care of the puppy. Reg stood there for some time watching the boy as he shut the puppy back in the kennel, and he was pleased when he saw John walk across to the huts and peep in at the chicks. He had not asked him to and it pleased him that the boy had used his own initiative.

CONSTANT VIGILANCE

Each morning John still went round the traps and snares. He had caught a stoat in one of the tunnels one day which had pleased him, but the vermin seemed harder to catch at this time of year. The grass and plants in the hedgerows were growing quickly and it was difficult to find time to keep the snares trimmed out. The weather was warm and sunny and when the chicks were three days old Reg let them have a small area of grass in the night shelter during the warmest part of the day. How John had laughed when they ran out of the hut and busied themselves pecking at the grass and leaping up to peck at marks on the boards. John had put his hand amongst them and several had been inquisitive and pecked at his fingers and his watch. When he moved they had run back into the safety of the hut. The first few days the chicks needed a lot of attention; once they were let outside a constant watch had to be kept on them if the temperature dropped. The second afternoon it had come over cloudy at tea time, just before John went to feed them and he was surprised how quickly they had got cold and how stupidly they had huddled together outside instead of going back inside the warmth of the hut. He quickly put them back in and he was astonished at how soon they revived once they were under the heater.

The following week there were sufficient chicks to fill three more huts and besides having to feed and water these, and go round their snares, Reg and John continued to get the rearing field completed. There would be a total of twenty huts, each with a night shelter butted on and with thirty feet by thirty feet runs leading off the night shelters. These had corrugated plastic sheets for roofs and over the run was a net, fastened round the outsides to the sections and propped up in the middle with a pole.

Debeaking

The next lesson John had to learn was the art of debeaking. When the first batch were ten days old Reg announced that it was time to debeak them. He did not believe in waiting until they started pecking — prevention being better than cure in his book. Consequently after breakfast that morning, when the feeding and watering had been attended to, they set about the task.

John watched as Reg gently eased the hardboard that had been used when the chicks were first put on the field, into the hut and drove the chicks in behind it so that they were quite tightly penned. Next John passed him a three legged milking stool, which Reg gently placed amongst the chicks checking that none had been trapped, and equally gently he sat himself down on the stool. John then handed in the debeaker, handling it carefully as the blade was very hot. The power to heat it came from the landrover battery to which it was connected by leads held on with crocodile clips. He watched as Reg grabbed a chick, holding it in his hand, so that he could prise its beak open, he then held the tip of the top beak against the glowing blade and as he closed the blade down onto the beak an evil smelling cloud of smoke rose — reminding John of a trip he had while on holiday years ago to see the village blacksmith at work shoeing horses. Reg held up the chick for John to see, the tip of its top beak had been removed, the heat sealing it so there would be no bleeding. Only a fraction of the beak was cut off and Reg assured John that it was quite enough to do the trick, without distressing the chick in any way. He dropped it gently over the hardboard, separating it

Figure 5.8   De-beaking in Progress

from its companions and then continued with the rest. Reg through his years of experience was quick at debeaking and in no time, or so it seemed, he had completed the first hut full.

John helped Reg move everything on to the next hut and was taken aback when Reg told him that he had to do this lot.

Having accomplished the difficult task of placing himself on the stool amongst the chicks Reg handed him the debeaker. It took two attempts before John was able to grab a chick so that it was facing the right way in his hand. A few moments of fumbling and he had its beak open. Holding the beak onto the blade made John wince and Reg laughed at the expression on the boy's face. Inspecting it afterwards he commented,

"You'll have to take a bit more off than that else it won't be enough to stop them pecking — the beak soon grows again, and they've got to last until we bit them when they are three weeks old."

John's attempt satisfied Reg's standard but caused him to comment that at the speed John was doing them they would hardly get finished by tea time let alone dinner time. The older man lit his pipe and sat down in the grass, leaning back against the hut and enjoying the sunshine. Meanwhile, inside, besides finding the stool rather hard to sit on, John found it hot, stuffy and dusty. He did, however, get quicker doing them and although it took about three times as long to do them as Reg had done he was satisfied that he had completed the whole hut full. When he checked them a few minutes later he was surprised that they seemed not the least bit perturbed by their brutal treatment, in fact they were busy scratching about as though nothing had happened.

The following day it was time to transfer the next batch of eggs from the incubator to the hatchers. This was the first full sitting of eggs as the hen pheasants took three or four weeks before reaching full lay. This time there were enough eggs to fill all four Iron Clads. The hens had reached a peak lay in the first week of May when they had reached one hundred and eighty nine but now, much to John's relief, the eggs were coming down in numbers.

The following Tuesday when the chicks were counted out Reg found that they had hatched above average, which meant that he had about a hundred chicks more than he had estimated. He was faced with the dilemma of part filling another hut that he would need for a later hatch or putting an extra twenty five chicks in each of the four huts he had allocated for the week's hatch. He decided on the latter policy, but warned John to keep a special eye on them as overcrowding usually brought trouble in his experience.

John's second attempt at debeaking was a great improvement on his first and he was beginning to get the hang of it despite still being a lot slower than Reg but it continued to puzzle him how quickly Reg could handle the chicks with his large hands.

May had been a kind month for keepers, it had been warm with a little rain and plenty of sun. The hen pheasants had laid well and still looked fit despite the rigours of being penned; the eggs so far had hatched well and the chicks were doing fine. Any pheasants in the wild would have benefited from the weather, and any chicks that may have hatched off would have had a good start. John too looked well; he was suntanned and fit, no longer the gangling school boy of the previous summer and he was totally absorbed with the progress through the season.

Figure 5.9   Melanistic Chick 'They Look Like Magpies'.

The Growing Season
6

JUNE

Figure 6.1   The Woods in the Growing Season

THE GROWING SEASON

MONTH: **JUNE**

A WET MONTH

For all the promise May had made for a good season, June soon lowered
their hopes. The first week was cold and wet and for the wild birds this was a
critical time. Continuous cold, wet weather was a chick's worst enemy and
they stood little chance of survival in the wet vegetation. The grass was thick
and tall where it had been left for hay and where it had already been cut for
silage it had soon begun to grow again and any hens that had nested in these
particular fields were either mangled by the machinery or their nests had
been destroyed. The corn too was tall and coming into ear; the hedgerows
were also a profusion of growth. Every morning when John went round his
snares he had to dress up in waterproof clothing or get soaking wet.

Apart from the discomfort of going round his snares when it was wet,
John also found it difficult work on the rearing field. Feeding was a
problem, for if the crumbs were left in the wet for even a short time they
went to an unappetizing soggy mash, the chicks too were unhappy, staying
in the warmth of the brooder huts for much of the time and everything
seemed wet and dirty. The only consolation John could find was that the
chicks required less water than when it was hot.

FITTING 'BITS'

It was now time to 'bit' the oldest batch of chicks and Reg was soon
teaching John the technique. Armed with a small carton, a landing net, a
bowl full of plastic bits, the old milking stool, a bucket and a small circle of
wire netting about fifteen inches high Reg and John set off towards the first
hut.

"Right John — get them all driven out of the hut and I'll shut the pop
hole", said Reg. Having done this they both drove the poults back into the

night shelter from the open run.

John watched as Reg reached for his penknife and then proceeded to cut some square holes in the carton.

"The hole in the side is to fit against the pop hole and the one in the top is to put the birds in when they are done. That way the ones in the night shelter won't be able to get muddled up with those that we have done in the hut", Reg explained.

"Get in the night shelter and I will hand the stuff to you", he continued.

As soon as John stepped into the night shelter the young pheasants flew in all directions but after a minute or so they settled back down on the ground. Reg handed in the equipment and then got in himself.

"Right now, put the carton so the hole in the side is against the pop hole, we'll open the trap in a minute, that way when we drop them in through the hole in the top they can run straight into the hut. Put the stool here and the bucket upside down over there, you can sit on that, it's not as comfortable as the stool", said Reg as he placed the wire netting circle in between the stool and the bucket.

He cursed as a poult ran into the bowl containing the bits and scattered them out onto the ground.

"Your job is to scoop the birds up in the landing net and empty them into

Figure 6.2   Poult at Three Weeks Old fitted with Plastic Bit

the wire surround; don't overfill it but keep me supplied", instructed Reg as he picked up the bits.

John filled the netting circle easily and sat down.

"Come on lad, I'll show you how to do it", said Reg as he picked up one of the small white oval shaped bits and caught a poult with the other hand. "You open its beak like you were debeaking and then fit one end of the bit into its nostril, then push it into place in the other nostril so that it lays inside the birds beak, preventing it from completely closing it." Holding it up for John to see he continued:

"You see, the tips of the top and bottom of the beak are kept apart, making it impossible for them to grip the feathers and pull them out."

John fumbled about with the first bird he did, but eventually the bit was in place to Reg's satisfaction. Although John thought he would never got the hang of this particular job it was not very long before he had got the knack, although he was nowhere as quick as Reg. At first the birds in the night shelter were easy to catch, but as their numbers dwindled it became increasingly difficult. Although small they could move very fast, and the night shelter roof was not high enough to stand upright which necessitated either trying to catch them bent over or kneeling down.

Eventually the last one was done and the equipment moved along to the other hut. Reg opened the door of the hut they had just done and John looking in felt sorry for the poults trying to rid their beaks of the bits, either by scratching at them with their feet or by wiping their beaks on floor.

"They don't like that much do they?" commented John.

"They shouldn't pull their feathers out and then it wouldn't be necessary", answered Reg. He looked thoughtfully in at the young poults. These early ones had done well and now at three weeks old they had lost nearly all their fluff and were clad in their juvenile feathers, identical in colouring to a hen pheasant. In a few more weeks they would change their plumage again; the hens would retain a similar colour and the cock birds would gradually gain their adult plumage. Apart from one odd bird that had accidently drowned in the water and two that had smothered, the losses had been low. As usual a few had died after the first week; these were ones that never seemed to grow properly, but after that the losses were negligible. Reg was pleased to see when he handled them that none was feather picked because although he kept a careful watch on them it was sometimes difficult to see when they started. Quite often the poults would start picking on the back feathers and if they kept their wings folded up it was very difficult to see this.

By lunch time both huts were finished and John went off to pick up the eggs while Reg looked round the rest of the chicks, already the birds were getting used to the bits and Reg knew in no time they would have forgotten all about them.

Figure 6.3   View of Modern Rearing Field

LAYING SLOWS DOWN

The following week was the last week that they set eggs — after that the young pheasants would not mature quick enough to be ready for shooting. The hens were still laying quite a few eggs each day, but numbers were dropping steadily. Reg changed them from pellets to wheat as soon as he no longer wanted the eggs and they soon dropped right off lay. John found it a great relief that there were no more eggs to pick up and wash each evening. He had even got tired of eating pheasants eggs. Reg and he shared any that hadn't been suitable to set and John had been living on them fried, poached, boiled, scrambled and as omelettes. Mrs. Plummer had also used them for cakes, egg custards and egg and bacon flans all of which John had eaten his share of. It was therefore not surprising that it was nearly a month before he again fancied an egg. Although there were no eggs to collect there was more work than ever. Each week there were approximately four huts full of chicks hatching out, all of which besides needing the usual feeding and watering would also in turn need to be debeaked and later on bitted.

RELEASING STOCK BIRDS

One free afternoon that Reg managed to contrive they set about catching up the laying birds and releasing them back into their natural environment. They put some netting across a corner and fastened the top over for a little way, then they drove a few in and John caught them and handed them to Reg who removed the brails and put them into the crates. When they had got as many crates filled as they could get in the back of the landrover they took them out and released them at a wood in the middle of the shoot. Despite a whole afternoon at it there were still a lot of birds left in the pen; any hour they could find spare after that was spent in catching some more up. Despite having one wing fastened securely into the closed position by the brail, once it was removed they could fly well and Reg knew they would be able to fend for themselves; already the fields of winter barley were beginning to change from green to brown as the ears started to ripen.

As John fed round that evening he could not but help thinking that life at the moment was very similar to a circus act he had once seen. A man had come on and started to spin plates on top of long fixed canes, he kept putting new ones up and then had to rush back to the original ones and set them spinning again before they fell down. So it was with the chicks; each week there were fresh ones to look after and all the while the older ones still needed attention. With the incubator still full of eggs there would certainly be no end to it for another month.

A FAMILY VISIT

One Sunday John's family had arranged to come and visit him. They planned to arrive early afternoon and Mrs. Plummer, wishing to meet them, had offered to provide them with tea. John hoped his mum and Mrs. Plummer wouldn't spend all afternoon comparing notes about him, but it would be good to see them again.

The day was warm and sunny and John had got as much of his work done in the morning as he could so he could spend the afternoon with his family. The first thing they were shown when they arrived was Sally; of course his brothers wanted to let her out and play with her but she was soon put back into the kennel when she laddered his mum's tights. Next he took them into the caravan and made them a cup of tea. His youngest brother was soon poking in the cupboards and John was quick to tell him off fearing the worst if he should touch anything when he showed them in the incubator shed. They sat and chatted for a while, John eager to find out any news of his old friends and school mates at home and his mum reassuring herself that he was well and happy.

When his mum had washed the cups up John took them on a guided tour of the incubator shed and the rearing field, explaining in detail what was involved, even his little brother was interested enough to stop getting into mischief.

The tour over Mrs. Plummer called out for them to come in as tea was ready. John awkwardly introduced his family to Mr. and Mrs. Plummer and soon they were busy chatting. Mrs. Plummer had laid on a magnificent spread in their little used dining room. John had seen the room, but never actually been in it before and was compelled to look in the china cabinet as he walked past. She had quite a collection of engraved glasses and ornaments, mostly of animals and birds. His mother meanwhile had taken one look at the table and pronounced that she knew why he had grown since he had been at Stonelands. They sat down and ate the home grown salad and home made scones and strawberry jam followed with home made cakes, all of which was delicious. Even his little brother remembered his manners and John began to relax. While his mother helped Mrs. Plummer clear away and wash up his father and Reg chatted; they seemed to be getting along well to John's surprise as his father knew little of the countryside and Reg knew no other way of life.

He took his brothers out to play with Sally again and to show them Reg's ferrets and chickens. After a while Reg came out and asked them if they would like a ride in the landrover as he was going to show John's father round the estate. John's brother thought it was great fun in the back of the landrover bumping along the tracks and across the fields. Soon, however, it was time to get back and to start the evening's chores. John's family had to leave as well as they had a long drive home. Before they were out of sight along the road Reg and John were making a start on the feeding and watering.

There were quite a lot of chicks now that were left out until dusk, and soon, when the nights were fine, they would be old enough to leave out all night, but, until then, and afterwards if it was likely to rain, they needed to be driven in. Once the chicks started to settle down in small groups as night drew on they were difficult to move, seemingly determined to remain outside in the places they had chosen, even though they would probably die from exposure if they were left out. The light was fading by the time Reg and John had finished feeding, watering and shutting the little ones in and John soon realised how stupid the poults could be.

MID-SEASON TIREDNESS

By the end of the month John was beginning to feel weary and consequently somewhat short tempered at times. Reg let the chicks out first thing, but, even so, John was outside at seven o'clock every morning, seven days a week and every evening he had to help shut up. Apart from the afternoon when his parents had come to visit he had not had any time off for weeks. He thought of his friends working at jobs that gave them evenings and weekends free to enjoy the summer; the ones that did have to work overtime, at least got paid for what they did. He was expected, in fact he felt, that Reg seemed to take it for granted that he would spend nearly every waking hour caring for the young pheasants.

One evening, when Reg was having a customary look round before going to bed, he discovered that John had forgotten to light one of the gas brooders. It had been a hot day and the three oldest lots of chicks had the heat turned off. There were nine huts altogether and somehow John had only lit the heaters in eight of them. Luckily no harm was done because the night was warm, but it could well have meant the loss of a hundred poults if the night had been cold and Reg had not taken his usual last look round.

The next morning Reg felt compelled to tell John off, although he understood only too well how the lad must be feeling. Indeed, he himself was feeling tired and jaded, but it was too serious a thing to leave unmentioned and it would not benefit the lad to ignore it; a warning would probably make him more conscientious in future.

John that evening was feeling very depressed, he was upset that he had neglected something important and that Reg had told him off. He was so tired he lay down on the bed with his work clothes on and it was one o'clock in the morning when he suddenly awoke. He got up with great effort and made himself a mug of coffee and then laid down on the bed again. He lay thinking over the last few months, realising that until recently he had very

Figure 6.4   Top of Gas Cylinder Showing Regulator and Heater

much enjoyed the work and so he drifted back to sleep. The alarm rung shrilly at half past six and he leapt up still fully clothed he knocked the mug of cold coffee off the table and all over the floor. He sat down on the side of the bed, forcing his eyes to stay open — another day had started, perhaps July would be a better month.

The
Game Fair
7

JULY

Figure 7.1   Game Fair: Dog Trial Finals   **Photo: Carter News Agency**

THE GAME FAIR

MONTH: JULY

John walked out of the caravan still feeling depressed. Reg came across to him, calling out a cheery good morning. At least he is not still cross with me thought John feeling a bit happier.

"I was thinking lad", said Reg. "I know you've been tired lately and there's been a lot to do; there'll be another two or three busy weeks yet so I think you ought to pull up your snares and spring your traps for a while. There's never much about at this time of the year with the crops still standing. You want to set them up again when the corn is cut; vermin will be on the move again then."

"Yes, I suppose it's a good idea — I haven't caught much lately", answered John, slightly disappointed because he enjoyed going round them each morning, but realising that it should ease the pressure of work a little.

"You pull 'em up for a month or so, you'll have birds in your pen before long and you'll need to set some round your pen then", Reg said.

"Another thing," continued Reg, "the keepers on the next door estate are planning to go to the Game Fair at the end of the month. I'm going with Fred the head keeper one day and his underkeeper Bob wondered if you'd like to go with him another day."

"Yes, I should love to go — I've never been to a Game Fair before only the smaller shows — where is it held this year?"

"It's in Wiltshire, quite a drive from here, but it's not likely to be any closer for the next few years", answered Reg. "I haven't been for several years."

John set off round his snares with a happier feeling inside him. It took a while to pull the snares up so that nothing could get accidentally caught; the traps were easier, he left them in position and flipped the safety catch over so that they could not spring shut. He was late back for breakfast and by the time he went outside again Reg had finished the feeding and was just starting the watering, he called out to John.

COCCIDIOSIS

"Those chicks in the tenth hut don't look too well to me — I think they've got a touch of coccidiosis — come and have a look."

John could see as soon as he opened the door that something was wrong — instead of running out into the night shelter they stood humped up, their wings hanging low and their feathers puffed up seeking the warmth of the heater. Reg had laid three dead ones on top of the hut and when John felt them they were thin.

"I've got some medicine for them over in the shed — it's in a yellow container on the bench, could you go and fetch it please?" Reg asked.

When John returned, Reg tipped the water out of the drinkers and filled a bucket with fresh water. He then carefully measured out the required amount of medication in the cap from the container and added it to the water, mixing it well in with his hand.

"We'll keep them on this for a few days — that should do the trick. With all this wet weather we've been having it's surprising we haven't had trouble before, but you'd better keep an extra eye on them. By the way if you mix this stuff up always add it to the water, if you pour water onto it it froths up and you can't see what you're doing for bubbles", Reg warned him.

The chicks soon responded to treatment and in a few days were back to normal although John noticed that there were several that looked as though they hadn't grown for the few days, giving the whole batch the appearance of being uneven in size.

THE FIRST POULTS

The first few days of July were very hectic because the first three huts that had been used were needed for the chicks that were due to hatch the following week; it was the last hatch, but it meant a rush getting the poults to wood. Reg explained that the first two huts, which were the oldest ones, would be used to fill a pen that Reg looked after on part of the estate that was farmed by a tenant farmer. It was at the far end of the shoot and Reg always put the oldest birds out there as they would be ready to shoot on the two smaller outside days they had before they started shooting the main woods later in November. With the third hut Reg intended to leave the poults in the run and night shelter, moving the hut to some fresh ground. The tiny chicks could manage without the night shelter for a few days and by the time it was necessary the older poults would have been taken to wood. Reg preferred doing this than to putting them into the release pens too soon — he always felt that the older they were when they were taken off the rearing field the better they survived in the wood.

The weather had looked uncertain when Reg intended to take the oldest poults to wood, and it was Sunday before the weather forecast spoke of settled weather. John persuaded Roger the cowman's son to come along and help so as soon as the morning's chores were finished they all set to. John had to catch them in the night shelter and hand them out in fives to Roger, who held them while Reg removed the plastic bits and clipped a few feathers off the end of one wing. Roger than put them into the crates.

John found it hard catching — it was dusty and uncomfortable working under the low roof and his hands were scratched from the poults sharp claws. Nevertheless, by four o'clock they had both huts caught up and were letting the last few out of the crates into the pen. Reg, Roger and John sat on the crates they had just emptied and watched the young pheasants as they inspected their new surroundings. Some had jumped out of the crates when the lids were slid back, but some had to be caught and lifted out. What a difference there was to the little stripey chicks that had been put into the huts a few weeks earlier. The cock birds were beginning to grow their adult plumage, some were already showing red on their heads around their eyes. Reg had placed the crates near some bushes so that when the birds were released they would have some cover nearby to hide in, making it less likely for them to try and fly, although they would be unlikely, with one wing clipped to be able to gain enough height to get over the wire netting.

Figure 7.2   Healthy Poults at Six Weeks

Feeding the poults

The keepers and their helper got up and walked quietly round the pen; already some of the birds were dust bathing in the dry soil under a fallen tree. When they had completed the circle John and Roger loaded the crates back onto the landrover while Reg filled a bucket with pellets from the feed bin near the pen gate and walked round again scattering the pellets where the young pheasants could easily find them. He checked that the drinkers he had filled the day before were still full and then fastened the gate securely behind him and bent down to switch the electric fencer on, the light on the unit flashed and it ticked as the electric pulse went along the wire. He knelt on one knee and showed John how to use a blade of grass to test the fencer without getting the full impact of the shock. The grass resisted the current so that only a small tickle could be felt instead of the full impact; even so John was very cautious when Reg made him hold it on the wire himself. He knew what a kick they gave because it was not long before that he had accidentally touched the fencer across the field where the cows were being strip grazed.

"Come on you two, it's tea time, and there's a lot of work still to do yet — I'll come and have another look at these later this evening", Reg called to Roger and John as he turned to get in the landrover.

THE FINAL HATCH

The days flew by, the last eggs hatched and it was with great relief that John scrubbed clean the equipment and put the trays back knowing that they would not be used again until the following spring. Once these last chicks were put on the rearing field John knew that the numbers would be getting smaller as each batch of pheasants got old enough to be put in the wood. John had the next two ages in his pen, six hut fulls in total. Although the two lots were a week different in age Reg put them all to wood over a period of three days so that the older ones were less likely to bully the younger ones not having had too long to make themselves at home before the addition of the smaller birds.

AROUND AND ABOUT

John enjoyed having birds in the wood; he set a few snares up round the pen and one or two tunnel traps where he could find suitable places. At first he gave the poults plenty of food but as they settled down he gradually decreased the food until they would run up to him when he went to feed them. He whistled as he threw the pellets out of the bucket and they would very soon connect his whistle with being fed so that when they were given their freedom they would still come in to feed. Gradually he mixed a

Figure 7.3   Feather Picking Illustrated

little wheat in with the pellets; in time this would be all they were given to eat except perhaps a little maize. At first the poults would not eat it, but after several days they would clear it up, but they always ate the pellets first and would run along behind him pecking up the pellets and ignoring the wheat until all the pellets were gone. They ate the greenstuff in the pen too, they loved nettles and the bracken and other foliage slowly disappeared as well wherever they could reach it. John would sometimes break or bend some hazel sticks over for them and they would descend on the leaves. John was happy again working in the woods; he fed twice a day, when the sun was up in the morning and when it was beginning to set in the evenings. Some evenings he would sit on an old fallen tree and watch the poults; every night he walked round the electric fence and checked it, occasionally a stem of bracken would fall across the wire impairing its efficiency and one evening a large piece of dead wood had fallen across it, pushing it onto the ground making it completely ineffective.

The last hatch of chicks were debeaked and the next pen to be filled was Reg's main pen. The weather was better than June had been although it was still unsettled, one or two days would be warm and sunny and then there would be a few days of showery weather, providing these weren't too heavy Reg welcomed them, as it gave the poults a chance to get acclimatized to the weather without getting too wet. While the weather was satisfactory for Reg it was a nightmare for the farm manager who was still trying to get some good hay made for the cows and youngstock the following winter.

THE GAME FAIR

John was looking forward to his day out at the Game Fair. Roger had asked if he could come along as well which had pleased John because he hardly knew Bob, Fred's under-keeper, and would have preferred the company of a friend.

Reg and Mrs. Plummer were going the day before with Fred and his wife and John was to be left in charge. There would be little chance of taking it easy though because besides his own pen and the rearing field to tend he also had the two pens of Reg's that now had birds in.

As Reg went across to the garage to get his car he was pleased to see John was already letting the poults out; the dew hung heavily on the nets and soon his hair and collar were wet. He watched as the Plummers drove off down the road, satisfied that Reg trusted him to care for everything in his absence. John had also been trusted with the landrover; although he could not yet drive it on the road, he could take it along the farm tracks which would be useful as one of Reg's pens was at least a mile away from the house. John was quite used to driving it now, he often used it to take bags of crumbs or pellets out to the rearing field if Reg wasn't needing it and since he had bought his moped he had also browsed through the Highway Code. Yes, he thought — I really must do something about having lessons and putting in for a test. With these thoughts in his mind he continued with the day's chores. First he fed the pens, then he had breakfast, next he fed and watered the birds on the rearing field. He occupied himself for the rest of the day with dismantling the pens that were now empty and stacking the sections in neat piles, ready to be picked up with the trailer when it was available.

In no time at all it was time to start on the feeding and watering again. By the time he had finished the sun was already low in the sky but it would be a fine warm night so only a few of the youngest would need shutting in. Luckily Roger drove into the yard as he was setting off so between them they soon had the birds driven in. By the time he had let Sally out for a run it was dark and all he had time for when Roger had left was a shower, for he did not want to be late in the morning. Bob had arranged to pick them up very early. The dogs started to bark just after he had turned the lights off, but when he listened he heard Reg's car pull into the garage and he felt a twinge of excitement when he thought about tomorrow.

He awoke before the alarm rang; it was quarter past five and Bob would be along to pick him and Roger up at six o'clock. He washed and dressed; what a change to be putting some smart clean clothes on; he was just finishing his breakfast when Roger put his head round the door.

"You're early, it's only quarter to", said John.

"I got dad to get me up when he went out to get the cows in otherwise I probably wouldn't have been", answered Roger. "I'll have a mug of tea if you can spare one", he continued.

"Help yourself", answered John as he went over to the cupboard by his bed and found some money to put in his wallet.

They were waiting out by the gate when Reg came out of his house.

"Glad I've seen you", he shouted across, "I've got the programme here you might as well take it, it'll save you a bob or two."

"Thanks very much", answered John, walking across and taking the programme. "Did you enjoy yourself?"

"Yes, thanks — but it was very hot and crowded. Was everything all right here?" asked Reg.

"Yes, except that it took me nearly all day to get round — I didn't have time to get many sections taken down. By the way do you think you could feed Sally for me, I've left her food mixed up ready in the shed, half for this morning and half for tonight."

"Of course I will — I hadn't forgotten — you asked me the other day. Now you get yourself off and enjoy yourself — forget about the work for a day", Reg said. "Looks like Bob's coming now — have a good time."

The car pulled up outside the gate and Roger and John climbed into the back. Bob introduced his wife Ann to them, she was sitting in the front seat. As she turned round and smiled at them John thought he had never seen a keeper's wife who looked less like a keeper's wife. She had long red nails, too much make up, a fancy hair do and very, very tight jeans. John found Bob's appearance equally interesting for he was dressed in a thick tweed keeper's suit and leather boots. Already the sun was breaking through the early morning mist promising a scorching hot day. Roger caught John's eye as he turned and they grinned at each other sharing the same thoughts.

They settled down in the back seat and were soon chatting with the exception of Ann who John thought probably could not tell a cock from a hen anyway. They talked of the present rearing season, and of shooting days past and future. The time and the miles sped by and Bob suggested that they should stop for some breakfast at the next service station they came to on the motorway. The egg, bacon and sausage was expensive and greasy and was not as nice as that which John cooked for himself most mornings. Bob and Ann appeared to enjoy the food and to find no fault with it causing Roger to remark in a whisper to John that perhaps she could not cook either!

They were soon heading along the motorway again and it wasn't long before they saw the first signs directing them off the motorway and onto the by-roads.

There were already rows and rows of cars parked across the field, shimmering in the bright sunshine. The gateway where they drove in was a dust bowl and the men taking the money at the gates were already covered in dust. Once through they were signalled along until finally they were waved into line beside another car — a continuous stream of cars followed them until very soon a fresh line was started.

"Hope I can remember where I've left it", said Bob. "It's not only finding it in this lot but there's probably two or three more car parks similar to this one."

They all looked round to familiarize themselves with the position. John nudged Roger and pointed to one woman in the next line who was busy tying her scarf to the aerial of her mini — perhaps it wasn't such a silly idea after all.

Their attention turned to Bob as he spoke.

"I think the best bet will be if we meet up at say five o'clock outside of the British Field Sports Society stand — we should all know where that is by five o'clock. We might not see each other again all day; it looks as though it will be packed.

"O.K. I think that's a good idea", answered John. "See you at five o'clock then."

With that Roger and John set off for the entrance, checking on the plan in the programme as they walked along as to which car park they were in.

Once through the turnstile they again looked at the programme and discussed what they particularly wanted to see. Their interests were similar so they decided to spend the day together and accordingly set off for Gunmakers' Row. They browsed through the stands marvelling at the superb displays of craftsmanship and the variety of guns on show and for sale. They watched carefully at the intricate designs of the engraver and the skill of the stocker. They rummaged through the piles of paraphernalia available on the stands; there was shooting equipment, knives, clothing and hats. John tried on an assortment of hats.

"Stop laughing will you", he shouted at Roger, "I've got to get one for a shoot day — Reg said and you are not much help to me choosing one."

"Come on, let's go and have a look at something else — we'll get you a hat later," answered Roger hurrying off causing John to run after him lest they got separated in the crowd.

Neither intended to stop as they walked along the next avenue, but both found the paintings and models worth a glance, such was the detail. They stopped too when they came upon a display of taxidermy. There were heads of deer, stuffed pheasants, partridges and foxes and a host of smaller mammals and birds. Two cases contained stoats either playing or fighting and arranged as they were in grass and dead leaves and some tree bark; it was difficult to believe they were no longer alive.

Reaching the end of the avenue they saw a great lake in front of him and towering above it the mansion. Archery demonstrations were taking place on the lawn between the mansion and the lake, and farther along was a falconer displaying the prowess of his bird, the whole scene lending a medieval air to the setting. In the foreground were the fishermen, lined along the edge of the lake. There were demonstrations for the newcomers and competitions for the more experienced. Hoops laid out in the water tested their skills as they attempted to cast the fly into the centre of each hoop — the experts made it look easy and the novices made it look difficult.

Parallel to the edge of the lake was another line of stands, displaying articles that were in any way connected with fishing. There were the usual assortment of clothing and boots and all the paraphernalia to equip the fisherman. There were rods by the hundred; all lengths and sizes, there were thick cane ones and thin fibre glass ones. Along with these were a colourful array of floats and flies, hooks and reels. On one stand was a young man demonstrating the art of fly tying. A few hairs, a few slivers of feather and a lot of patience and he soon had a hook adorned with the manmade fly that would deceive all but the wiliest of fish.

Walking on from Fisherman's Row, John and Roger discussed their personal experiences of fishing and discovered that they had both spent more time unravelling birds nests from the line and evading being caught by angry water bailiffs or river keepers than they actually had catching fish.

They spotted a refreshment marquee and joined the queue, eventually coming away with a couple of cans of coke and some cheese rolls. Finding a space in the shade of a tree on the edge of the lake they sat down to enjoy their refreshments. The Game Fair was a noisy place. Besides the general hubbub of the people and children there were the sound of shots and whistles coming from the gundog tests and demonstrations farther along the lake; away in the distance was the continual barrage of shots from the clay shooting section and overhead the whirring of helicopters as they landed and took off on their ten minute joy rides over the estate. Although Roger was not particularly interested in dogs he was happy to accompany John as he made his way along to watch the gun dogs in action.

They watched as beautifully trained labradors went through the tests, retrieving dummies from the rough grass and vegetation along the edge of the lake and the water itself. A long blast on the handlers whistle would stop the dog from its quest and hand signals from the handler would send it off again in the right direction so that it returned successfully to the owner carrying the dummy gently in its mouth. Occasionally a dog would disobey its commands, but John had never seen dogs so well trained and he noted the difference in their styles, some would go very quickly whilst others plodded around, but one thing John did notice was that every dog enjoyed what it was doing. Not far from the labradors was a competition that any

Figure 7.4   Goshawks are a Feature of the Game Fair

visitors could enter with their gundogs. This was called a **scurry** and involved the dog fetching two dummies, one from the rough grass and one from the water, the winner being the one that did it in the fastest time. John and Roger both found this fun to watch as there was an assortment of breeds and a certain variation in the quality of training. Before leaving the dog section they looked round the tents housing examples of the different gun dog breeds to be found in this country and also hounds.

They continued making their way around the never ending lines of trade stands and demonstrations. Along Game Farmers' Row were chicks and poults and an assortment of rearing equipment and accessories. There were stands selling kitchen tools, jewellery, tea towels and books; there were complete pet shops selling everyting from flea powder to choke chains, as well as forestry demonstrations, a **pugs and drummers** corner, displaying anything to do with rabbiting and in particular the ferret; in fact anything that was in the remotest way connected with field sports was well represented. They finished up near the pigeon plucking competition where the queue of people were waiting to try their hand at being the Pigeon Plucker of the year.

The time was three thirty and John and Roger went in search of some refreshments. Again there was a queue, but this time there was no shade for them to sit in, they both felt hot, tired and dusty and their feet ached and they agreed that this was harder than work. They had seen most of the show with the exception of the clay pigeon shooting and the main arena which was so crowded, being able to see much would have been an impossibility.

"I've seen one or two things I want to buy if I can remember where I've seen them", said John, flattening his empty coke tin. "Do you want to come with me or shall we meet up at five o'clock."

"I'll come with you — what do you want to get?" asked Roger.

"Well, I want some stuff for Sally, we'll go over to that stand there, they've got some stainless steel food bowls and a lead like I want. Then on one of the stands along Gunmakers' Row they've got a whistle and a penknife and I suppose I ought to get a hat really", answered John.

"I know, Reg is a stickler for appearance and manners — one day last season he told me off for turning up beating in one of my dad's old coats — mind you it did honk a bit of cows so I can't say I blamed him". You'll have to wear a tie and get your hair cut before you're allowed in front of the guns", Roger remarked.

They set off again through the crowds to make John's purchases, the hat being the most difficult choice to make. Roger thought the best one for John was a Sherlock Holmes' deer stalker complete with ear flaps tied up with ribbon, but John did not share his enthusiasm and did not think that Reg would either. John finally decided on a cap, which, while looking a little odd perched on his present mop of hair, thought would meet with Reg's approval once he had his hair cut.

They met up with Bob and Ann as arranged and headed towards the car park. Ann was still sporting quite a lot of make up although her hair style was slightly disarranged. Bob on the other hand was a light shade of red with beads of sweat standing out on his forehead, but still he wore his thick tweed jacket.

"Hot isn't it?" remarked Roger winking at John.

A continuous line of cars queued to leave the car park and above them a pall of dust hung in the air. Their own car was like an oven when they opened the doors and they discussed what they had seen while they waited for the car to cool down.

The time was past seven when they were heading back down the motorway and they chatted about their day. Bob had met up with a friend he had not seen for at least ten years and had spent some time exchanging news of other acquaintances.

He turned the car into the first pub that they came to once they had left the motorway. John was glad of a chance to wash the grime from his face and hands and then relax in the coolness of the bar with an ice cold shandy. They each ordered a steak and were soon enjoying the unaccustomed luxury.

Reg heard the car pull up and the door bang soon after he had gone to bed and he wondered whether John would be up in the morning. John was wondering the same thing as he turned out the light and laid down in bed.

The next morning, out on the rearing field, John thought about his day out; it seemed as though he had visited another planet so different was it from the peace and quiet of the Sussex countryside. How anyone could enjoy working in a crowd was beyond his comprehension, he certainly knew where he would sooner be; yet had enjoyed himself. Back to reality now though, there was the feeding and watering to do and the last batch of poults were due for bitting!

Dealing With
The Elements
8

AUGUST

Figure 8.1   Friend or Foe?

DEALING WITH THE ELEMENTS

MONTH: AUGUST

Work on the farm was at its peak, the whole estate was busy with the harvest. The combine harvesters slowly devoured the fields of golden barley, followed by the balers spitting out the bales ready for tractors and trailers to pick up and store away in the barn for use in the winter. The pressure of work for the keepers was easing; they were still busy, there was no longer quite the urgency. John found he could spare a little more time tending his pheasants. He carried a few bales of straw into his pen and scattered it along the feed ride. There was little in the pen left to occupy the young pheasants and they had started to pull out each others tail feathers. At first it had alarmed him, but Reg reassured him that nuisance that it was, it quite often happened and they would soon grow again once the birds spread out round the woods; even so John thought it definitely spoiled the birds appearance and determined to do all he could to keep them otherwise occupied.

THE PREDATOR

A sparrow hawk too had been causing him trouble; day after day it would come to his pen and kill a young pheasant but eventually he came upon it one evening when he had taken his gun with him* — protected or not no keeper could tolerate one returning so regularly to kill his poults.

John enjoyed feeding the pen now the poults were settled. They ran up to him when he whistled and some evenings he waited after he had fed them, he would sit and watch them go to roost. Quite a few still crouched on the ground, but the bolder ones would attempt to settle amongst the hazel branches although their attempts at getting in position were somewhat amateurish. Frequently they would miss their footing and return to the ground with a clatter.

***It is illegal to kill a sparrow hawk**

THE CHANGING WEATHER

The weather was still hot and humid and Reg was only too aware that this spell would end in a thunderstorm; meanwhile the combines had advanced into fields of wheat.

The storm arrived with a vengeance in the middle of the night, it thundered and lightened and the rain battered on Reg's bedroom window and on the roof of the caravan making sleep impossible for either. John got up and made himself a cup of tea and he saw Reg's kitchen light go on. He knew the older man would be worrying about the poults he had put to the wood a few days previously. A sudden flash of lightening and the lights went out and there was nothing to do but wait for it to get light. The storm rumbled about for the rest of the night; John heard the landrover go off as soon as it was light and he got up and dressed. It was still raining as he walked up the track towards his pen, the water had cut a gulley through the dirt where it had rushed along the track and the grass and branches were bowed over with the weight of the water on the leaves.

John reached the pen and looked round for his pheasants; they were hidden amongst the undergrowth and trees, trying to find some shelter. They stood upright in an effort to drain the water off their feathers, but surprisingly they came out to feed when he scattered some food along the

Figure 8.2 Type of Pheasant Food

ride. He looked round quickly and found two dead ones, neither were very big and would probably have died anyway.

John then hurried down to the rearing field, luckily having listened to the local weather forecast the evening before Reg had decided to shut them all in. The youngest he shut right in the huts and the rest just into the night shelters. He hurriedly let them out and as usual they ran or flew out of the gates to the far end of the runs where they busied themselves hunting through the grass for worms and slugs. The birds were nearly all dry except for an odd one that had settled down where the rain had driven in under the roof.

John walked round again when he had finished letting them out and checked the night shelters for dead ones. He found three in the corner of one and four in the corner of another; they were trampled flat on the ground and it was difficult to tell whether they had been smothered or whether the rain had caused their deaths.

Reg pulled into the field in the landrover as John was checking the last hut. He sat in the landrover while John walked across to him.

"How are these — and have you had a look up in the wood yet?" he asked as the lad reached him.

"I picked up seven here and I went up the wood earlier and found a couple — the others came up to feed o.k." John answered.

"That's not bad — bloody lucky we shut these in last night I bet some people didn't bother and suffered because of it", Reg remarked — he continued: "Mine are o.k. out Grove, but those we put in the Park last week don't look too good — there's several laid about, dead but I left them else I might disturb those that had found a bit of shelter — you'd better give me a hand later to look round — I hope to God it soon leaves off. Come on we'd better go and get some breakfast."

John peeled off his wet coat and leggings in the incubator shed and ran across to the caravan — he was soaked through and while the kettle boiled he quickly changed. He soon felt better with a hot breakfast inside him and especially so when he went back outside and found the rain easing as the sky brightened.

He went across to the landrover, Reg was just putting some empty paper feed bags in the back.

"Come on" he said "we'd better go and discover the worst — at least it's leaving off."

They splattered their way through the puddles along the track to the Park. A dismal sight greeted them as they pulled up near the gate — dark sodden shapes were huddled together, trying to gain shelter from the inadequate cover of bracken and stinging nettles. Several were humped up, their heads turned round over one shoulder and their beaks tucked into the top of one wing, they scarcely moved when John approached. An odd one was laid out on its side with no more than a glimmer of life left in it, only becoming apparent when it was picked up — perhaps there was a faint movement of the head or a leg, but few would recover from the prolonged exposure.

Reg handed John a paper bag and they criss-crossed the pen in their search for the dead. In half an hour they had picked up fifty and another dozen or so that were not quite dead. John felt as depressed as Reg looked, thinking of the care and worry that had gone into the rearing of the birds not to mention the expense.

Reg broke the silence: "Well, I suppose it could have been worse, if they had been younger or reared indoors like a lot of keepers have to rear their birds we'd have lost a lot more. There'll have been a lot of pheasants put to wood in the last week or two and I bet there's a lot of keepers who have suffered more than us."

Reg filled a bucket with pellets and walked round the pen whistling as he scattered the food — surprisingly quite a few of the birds came up to feed. Ironically as they threw the bags of dead ones into the back of the landrover the sun broke through and the woods suddenly sparkled in the sunlight.

They took the bags of dead to a pit that had been dug for them in the wood. A mangy old rat crept down a hole as they threw the bags in on top of the old eggshells and unhatched eggs from hatching time. The whole pit heaved with maggots and the stench hung in the damp air.

"I must get Martin to fill this in else we'll be overrun with rats — I put some poison down the other day and it's all gone*. Let's hope we don't have anything else to put in here", said Reg returning to the landrover.

When they reached home John went back up to his pen to give them some more food while Reg started to feed the poults still on the rearing field.

The food was all gone from the pen and the poults looked hungry. The pellets soon disintegrated in the wet so he had not given them much earlier. When he had approached the pen the young pheasants were all spread out in the sun drying; they were busy preening their feathers, but as soon as they heard him whistle they had run towards him.

After dinner Reg and John went back to the Park. Reg brought five poults back with him that had dried out under an infra-red lamp, the other seven they had taken home had died. John was surprised how quickly the birds in the pen had dried. They were running about as though the storm had never been, but when Reg had fed them they looked round again and picked up another ten cold, wet bodies.

FURTHER PROBLEMS

The few days that followed caused more anxiety; while the birds in the Park seemed fully recovered once the sun had shone again, a few days after

*** Poison would be hidden from view away from animals and birds.**

the storm some began to look unwell, their ruffled feathers and dejected appearance suggested to Reg that they had probably got coccidiosis brought about by the wet conditions, so the yellow container was unearthed again and the medication mixed up.

John too had problems at his pen. A few of the poults were strong enough to fly out and although the majority were still inside the safety of the netting the ones that were out were attracting the attention of a fox. The first night John had found three bodies, two had been bitten across the back and one had its head missing.

John searched the surrounding area, but could find no more and he asked Reg for the morning free to set some more snares. The next night the fox never called, but the night after it came and killed another nine. John felt very frustrated; there was little more he could do, apart from hanging a few bags up in the trees but Reg had little faith in this method of deterrent. He would have felt less bitter, but for the fact that the fox was only killing for fun. It had not eaten any of the birds John had found so far and it made him extra careful in checking the electric fence each day. If the fox got inside there was no telling how many it would kill. Reg had frightened John when he told him how a fox got into one of Fred's pens one year and killed one hundred and seventy five half grown poults in one night. He knew it was true because Reg himself had seen the sacks full of carcasses.

Reg came up to John's pen when he was feeding that evening and looked round at his snares; he could find no fault in how or where they were set and so he turned his attention to the birds in the pen. John tried to drive as many of the birds outside, back inside the pen at night. He patiently waited for them to find their way in the gates or through the specially designed grilles that would allow them access to the pen while denying the ones inside an exit. John marvelled at the inability of a pheasant to see a large hole into the pen while they could very easily see even the smallest hole out of it!

His mission completed he went over to sit beside Reg on the fallen tree where he was puffing thoughtfully away at his pipe.

"Now lad, just you be quiet a minute and listen", he said to John.

John listened; he could hear the little birds in the trees and a pigeon lazily cooing and the combine humming away in the distance, mosquitoes buzzed near his face and midges settled on his forehead and arms to bite him.

"There, did you hear that", Reg broke the noisy silence.

"No, what was it?" asked John.

"Look — watch that pheasant."

THE GAPES

John did as he was told and suddenly it shook its head and sneezed. John knew vaguely that it must have the **gapes.** He had heard his Uncle talk of it and some amazing old fashioned remedies that used to be applied.

"It's got the gapes hasn't it?" enquired John tentatively.

"Yes, there's another one over there as well", answered Reg. "It's caused by a threadlike worm that settles in the pheasant's windpipe, the bird sneezes in an attempt to dislodge it and if left untreated the windpipe gets so congested that the bird either suffocates or gets so weak that it is susceptible to any other disease that may be present. They've probably got it now because the slugs and worms act as a host to the gape-worm and are readily eaten by the pheasant especially when they appear in quantities when it is wet. The gape-worm can survive from year to year in a release pen so that if left untreated it can get progressively worse."

"How do you treat it?" asked John.

"You can either have a powder mixed in with the feed or else mix some stuff in with the water — either way it's darned expensive", Reg answered him. "I think we'll leave it for a day or two — if they get worse we'll have to treat them, it might be only an odd one that's got it though. Come on lad, the lecture's over — let's get back home."

John sat dejectedly in the landrover — a couple of weeks before everything had seemed fine and now everything was going wrong. He voiced his thoughts to Reg as he settled himself behind the steering wheel.

DISCUSSIONS ON KEEPERING

"That's keepering", Reg answered. "There's always something going wrong or trying to take the pheasants; this time of year it's the four legged predators. Once the birds are fully grown it will be the two-legged ones trying to make some easy money. You have to be continually pitting your wits against the problems. The men who can come part way to solving some of these problems are the good keepers, the ones who never even try are the bad keepers. By the way, changing the subject, it's about time you started to train your pup, she's six months old now, I know you've got a couple of books but if you want any advice you just ask."

John perked up at the mention of Sally; he knew she was in need of some discipline.

"I've read both of my books and they each say different things so perhaps I'd better follow your advice — Roger says your dogs work well and that you are strict about dogs out shooting.'

"Thanks for the compliment; if you take my advice the first thing you'll do is to get her walking sensibly on the lead, and secondly to walk sensibly off the lead. When you can do them properly I'll tell you what to do next — but always remember, you must perfect one lesson before you advance to the next."

Figure 8.3   A Strip of Artichokes which provide Excellent Cover

"You'll probably not find much of what I do in your books but I've found it gets results", continued Reg. "The dogs you saw working at the Game Fair are very well trained and they look good, but they would be little use to me if they kept looking for directions in the middle of our thick plantations. No, what I want is a dog that will work on its own initiative and behave itself at the same time. Tomorrow you get yourself a thin swishy hazel stick out of the hedge and put Sally on the lead. Don't use the stick to hit her, but wave it in front if she pulls ahead, if she drags behind pull her up into position at heel on your left side and keep on telling her to heel — she'll soon learn. I've found the stick useful for two reasons, it gives you a longer reach and it accustoms a dog to the stick when you're beating. It's surprising how alarmed a young dog can be when it's surrounded by men banging sticks against the hedges and trees."

"O.k., I'll try that and I'll do as you say", said John enthusiastically.

"You do that, and ask straight away if you have any problems", replied Reg.

The two keepers sat in the landrover for an hour discussing dogs and pheasants and it was dark by the time they returned home.

Next morning John was again upset to find that the fox had visited his pen once more, but his mood soon altered when he found a dog fox dead in one of his snares.

That evening he got Sally out of the kennel; she jumped about expecting the usual romp around the orchard before John fed her, but tonight she had a nasty shock when she discovered the lead around her neck. At first she went mad fighting the lead and leaping all over the place. She then dragged behind only to be jerked into position besides John's left knee; next she tried to pull ahead of him only to find herself jerked back and the stick waved in front of her face. After twenty minutes she had settled down quite well although she became unsettled again as he neared the kennels.

The next evening when he took her out along the track she soon settled to walking at heel, so John let the lead drop to the ground as he walked quickly along, ready to tread on it should he see any likelihood of her misbehaving and all the time commanding her to 'heel' punctuated with 'good girl' to reassure her.

During the next few lessons John progressed to letting her off the lead completely and starting to train her to sit. At first he had to keep pushing her firmly into position while commanding 'sit' and then to begin with the lead on and afterwards with it off he would walk a few paces backwards while giving the command and not allowing her to stand up until he was back standing beside her. He took her out every evening for about twenty minutes, repeating and perfecting what she had learned, before advancing to anything new. Reg came out with him one evening and sat on the gate quietly as the lad took the pup through her lesson. She was still rather playful, but when John got through to her that it was serious stuff she behaved quite well. He tried to forget Reg was watching as he walked along the track. He walked quickly and stopped several times commanding Sally to sit at once. Twice he walked away from her a few paces and then returned to her and each time she had stayed sitting. John walked back towards Reg and suddenly Sally rushed forward to greet him; John shouted but she took no notice much to his annoyance.

"Don't worry — she's coming along all right", said Reg, patting the young bitch as she wriggled round his legs, "Put her back on the lead; pups seem to be able to concentrate with one person, but two seems to excite them."

John did as he was told and they walked back to the house together.

"What shall I do now?" asked John.

"I should practise a bit more on what you've done — don't worry about retrieving yet, you've got to get her obedient first", Reg answered.

"What else can I do."

"Several things — to test how well she'll stay you can gradually lengthen the distance between you and keep saying **stay** and **sit** alternately. When she doesn't move try walking in a circle round her. At first she'll probably move when she can no longer turn her head round. If she does, firmly pick her up and put her back where you left her telling her to sit and stay. When you can walk a circle round her without her moving try hiding behind a tree for a few seconds. Again, if she moves, firmly put her back where you left her. Another thing you must do is to get her to come to you, but make sure she'll stay where you want before starting that. At first you want to walk away a few paces and then call her in. Don't forget to tell her what a good girl she is and fuss her when she comes to you; after that you can walk along giving the command **stay** while you keep walking and if she obeys you can call her in to heel without stopping. You must start to get her used to the whistle as well; blow a long blast whenever you command her to stay and several short blasts when you want her to come to you. Eventually she will obey the whistle or the vocal command but to start with do both. Two things you must remember; firstly, be certain that the puppy is perfect at one lesson before you advance to another and only try and teach her one thing at a time; she must know how to do that before you try anything else. Secondly, if you don't feel in tune with her or you feel you might lose your temper, put her straight back in the kennel. If you have a misunderstanding it could take weeks to gain her confidence again, it's far better to put her away."

"O.k. I'll try and remember all that but what about retrieving?" asked John impatient to be teaching Sally the job she was bred for.

"I don't think you'll have any trouble there", answered Reg, "She's always picking things up and carrying them around — I've seen a lot of dogs that will retrieve anything, but have never been taught any basic discipline and they're a bloody nuisance on a shoot day — no you be patient and lay

Figure 8.4 Jill Mason with Bob, Badger and Meg

the foundations right, the rest should fall into place after that."

August went by quickly. John had treated his pen with water medication for gapes and the birds had soon recovered. They were growing well and as their juvenile feathers moulted out so more flew out of the pen. The small wing feathers were replaced with larger ones and as the clipped feathers became fewer their effectiveness became less. John tried to drive as many as he could into the safety of the pen each evening, but they were growing more independent. Quite a number had lost their tails, but there were short blue quills showing through and their feathers were obviously growing again. John liked to watch the poults that were out as they searched the stubble for grain or dusted in the dry earth in the heat of the midday sun.

Sally was progressing well. She was sometimes over-exuberant, but she was still only a fat shiny puppy. Already a bond was forming between the two of them each aware of the others moods, a bond that hopefully would grow until they formed a partnership together.

The nights began to draw in and the leaves had lost the sticky dusty look they had during the long days; the combines were nearing the end of their short hectic spell of work and would soon be driven under the barn, greased up and put away for another ten or eleven months.

The rearing season was fading into a memory as the last of the poults were put to wood and the equipment dismantled. The worry and the long hours were forgotten as John watching his pheasants grow began to look forward to the shooting season.

The Tidying-up Month
9

SEPTEMBER

Figure 9.1   A Poult eating Greenstuff

THE TIDYING UP MONTH

MONTH: **SEPTEMBER**

September arrived and summer waned; no longer was the sun so hot despite the clear blue sky. The mornings were fresher and misty and the dew sparkled on the grass and on the intricate webs that the spiders had interlaced between leaves and twigs, grass and thistles. John thought back to the spring, how the yellow flowers had given way to the red and purple flowers of summer and now the flowers had changed to berries and fruits. Hips and haws and rowan shone red in the sun and the dark sloes and blackberries provided tempting pickings for the pheasants. Black too were the stubbles in the fields where they had been burned. The tractors were busy cultivating and ploughing and overhead beech masts and acorns ripened to entice the pheasants even farther away.

THE ROGUE DOG

One late afternoon, John was happily making his way to his pen when he stopped in his tracks; a dog was barking in the direction of his pen! He panicked as he saw the crossbred collie chase a young poult around the wire. He shouted and the dog stopped giving the pheasant a chance to fly over the wire, John called gently to the dog to come, but it took no notice; he walked towards it and the dog tucked its tail between its legs and skulked away from him. There was no way that he could catch hold of it on his own so he turned and ran as quickly as he could back home. He knew Reg would be feeding his pheasants so he got out his moped and went as fast as he could to the pen that he thought Reg was most likely at.

Reg was shutting the lid of the feed bin when he first heard the moped coming towards him through the wood. His birds scattered off the feed ride and he cursed.

"Whatever are you doing coming up here on that", Reg shouted angrily, but his voice softened as he saw the boy's face. "Whatever's the matter lad?"

"There's a killer dog in my pen, I saw two birds it had killed on the track and I couldn't catch the wretched thing — it's still in there", he answered with a trembling voice.

"Steady on — it'll do no good getting so upset", Reg told him, but John noticed that as he spoke his face tightened and his eyes hardened. "Come on, hop in we'd better get out there as quick as we can."

The landrover lurched its way quickly through the woods, neither spoke.

"Hell — there's always something trying to get the pheasants — every time there's a few less to put over the guns" Reg spoke angrily as they neared the wood.

They hurried into the pen and stopped to listen; a commotion at the farthest end of the pen betrayed the dog's presence, even as they stood there the young pheasants ran and flew low past them. Suddenly the dog broke the cover and stopped when it saw the men.

"I've had trouble with that dog before; I let it out of a snare a few weeks ago — I wish to God I hadn't now", Reg spoke bitterly. He walked back to the landrover and reached behind the seat for his gun. He checked his pocket for cartridges and placing two inside the barrels he returned to John. They walked towards where they could hear the dog, and as it stopped when it saw them Reg raised the gun, slipped the safety off and fired. The shot echoed round the woods ringing in John's ears and the dog lay quivering on the leaves, blood spurting from its head.*

"Sorry lad — I had to do it", said Reg quietly sensing the boy's feelings. "It's the owner that ought to be shot not the dog. I expect it comes from the village."

"I don't know how many it's killed. I saw two earlier but there don't seem to be hardly any left in the pen", said John dismally.

"We'd better have a look round, luckily it's a big pen and the birds are well grown so hopefully they have either flown out or are laying low", Reg answered.

The Slaughter

They walked round the pen and picked up seven bodies — they were nearly big enough to eat and it seemed such a waste. They saw several skulking in the brambles, their scared beady eyes warily watching the men as they flattened themselves into the ground. Completing the circle Reg took hold of one of the dogs hind legs and dragged its body out of the gate.

"Get a paper bag out of the back of the landrover", Reg instructed John.

He put the body inside the bag and threw the dead pheasants in on top.

***This should not be construed that keepers normally kill dogs or that it is a legal act, although it is *legal* to shoot a dog worrying livestock inside a pen, providing there is no other way to stop it and the identity of the dog is unknown (Section 9, *Animals Act,* 1971).**

"Won't you get into trouble?" John asked, feeling wretched that someone's pet had died because of him.

"I might do", Reg answered, "don't you go saying anything about it to anyone. More often than not you don't hear anything more. People who let their dogs roam wild care little for their welfare anyway — for all they know it may have been hit by a car or got on the railway line on the other side of the village. They never believe that their pet could be killing or chasing anything, it's not just pheasants and rabbits you know — it's cattle and sheep and deer as well. I've taken dogs caught in snares into the local police, the owner pays the fine or costs or whatever it is and a few days later the dog is back on the estate again. After all a dog is only doing what comes naturally to him, hunting. No, it's the owners who need shooting not the dogs."

John knew what Reg meant, he himself felt angry when he saw people noisily walking along the footpaths allowing their dogs to run about in the woods ignorant of the damage and disturbance they were causing and destroying the very thing they came to enjoy. Reg's voice broke into John's thoughts.

"You'd better chuck them some grub around, feed inside and outside the pen, the best thing to do is to leave them quiet to settle down I'll come with you in the morning and we'll see what damage it's done."

John whistled as he fed but not one bird showed itself. Reg threw the bag in the back of the landrover and checked the electric fence — it wasn't working so he set off round to find out the fault — he had not gone far when he found a dead branch had fallen across the netting and onto the electric fence rendering it useless. He lifted the branch off as best he could and pulled the netting back up, he tightened the electric fence wire up and soon it was working again.

"You were unlucky — the branch had knocked the wire and the fence down and the dog came along the same day", Reg remarked. "You do check the electric fence every day don't you?"

"Yes", John answered quietly his misery deepened with the realization that Reg had thought to doubt him.

"We'd better get rid of the dog", said Reg.

"What are you going to do with it?" asked John.

"Put it down the well at the derelict cottage up in Top Wood; it won't be the first to be put in there and probably not the last", Reg answered sadly.

GETTING THE BIRDS SETTLED

Several days passed before John's pheasants settled down again and there certainly weren't the number there that there had been before the dog's visit. It was useless trying to get them back inside the pen so Reg and John had lifted some of the netting and opened the gate wide so that the birds

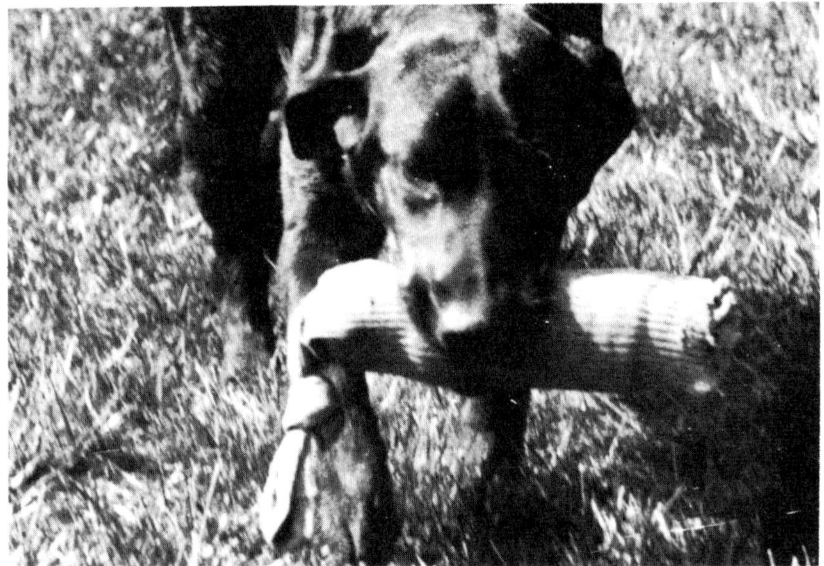

Figure 9.2   Sally Training

could easily pass to and fro.

John spent time most mornings setting his line of snares and traps again and he noticed that small groups of his pheasants were beginning to explore the hedge rows. It quite alarmed him to see how far some of them were away from the pen and he spent much time driving them back towards home. He tried to walk them quietly back up the hedges but if they were out across the fields he would run at them shouting and waving his arms all the while hoping that no one was watching his antics. Reg too spent a lot of his day driving in, although his youngest poults were still safely in the pen. He took one of his dogs who soon chased them back home until he called her back. If she caught one she would return to him carrying it tenderly in her mouth causing Reg to curse as it meant he had to take it back to the pen himself. He wished he could train her not to catch them except when he wanted her to but he could not work out how to do it.

DOG TRAINING CONTINUES

Sally's training was progressing. John had started her on retrieving; he made a dummy as Reg had instructed of a small log of wood wrapped in a piece of foam rubber and wrapped in a sock. She had readily fetched it to him once she knew what was wanted, but was in the habit of spitting it out at his feet instead of holding it in her mouth for him to take hold of. Reg's advice had been to run away from her as soon as she returned with the dummy so that she would continue carrying it and then John could take it from her before she had time to think about dropping it. John practised it two or three times every evening and slowly Sally improved.

TIDYING UP

September was what Reg called a tidying up month. He and John spent most afternoons getting the rearing equipment cleaned and stacked neatly away in readiness for the following Spring. Later on in the month there would be all the feed rides to trim out; the nettles, bracken and grass would need to be trimmed short and the overhanging branches cut back making the feed rides light and clear to feed the pheasants on. At present they were still only feeding at their pens, but as the birds matured and spread out farther away the need would soon arise to feed them out in the surrounding coverts and game cover. To hold them in the drives they would shoot and hopefully prevent them straying onto their neighbours estates. As well as the places John had fed when he started at Stonelands, the previous February, he would have to have two additional feeds. There was the plantation flanked by a row of silver birches which he had previously been told not to feed and a strip of kale that Mr. Brinklow had promised would be left from the ten acre field that the cows would soon be starting on. It was between the Pen Wood and Smiths and would make a useful extra drive.

FOXES AND A STRAY DEER

John was pleased with himself for catching three foxes in ten days. Reg had told him they would be moving now the corn was cut but he hadn't expected to catch that many so quickly. His pleasure was marred slightly one morning by finding a roe deer dead in one of his snares.* It lay under a three strand barbed wire fence and he could not understand why it had chosen to squeeze through the twelve inch gap under the wire in preference to jumping over the top. Agile as the deer were it was incomprehensible that it had chosen to wriggle itself under such a small gap. There was no sign of a struggle and the snare was tight round its neck; most likely the deer had died from fright than through strangulation. Reg and he fetched it in the landrover, but before they loaded it into the back Reg made John gut it.

"You'll have to go careful because it's blown up as tight as a drum — if you pierce its stomach all the contents will spill out and it'll stink to high heaven", said Reg, as he handed John his sharp penknife and stepped back up wind.

***Constant care and vigilance are necessary to avoid accidents of this type: it is illegal to set snares for deer.**

Figure 9.3   Skinned Roe Deer

"Just do the gutting as you would a rabbit, but cut through the windpipe in its neck, then when you pull its lungs out the windpipe will come too" Reg continued.

He watched as John gingerly set about gutting it, very carefully slitting the skin and easing out the intestines. It smelt sweet and sickly and the congealed blood spilled out on the grass from around it's heart. Reg salvaged the liver and kidneys for his dinner and the heart and the lungs for his dog's supper, the rest they threw in the hedge. Having gralloched his first deer, John had to learn how to skin the animal when they got back to the house. He was surprised how easy it was once they had got the deer hung up by its hind feet and had slit the skin up the inside of the hind legs.

John had just got back to his caravan and was endeavouring to rid his hands of the smell when Reg knocked on the door.

"I've left it hanging in the shed and I put the skin and head in a paper bag", John told him.

DRIVING LESSONS ARE ARRANGED

"O.k. — it's not that I wanted to see you about — I've booked you in for a driving lesson next Wednesday afternoon; the chap will pick you up at two o'clock. If you don't want to go you'll have to let him know", Reg said. "If you take my advice you'll have lessons and soon get put in for a test — a keeper's not much good these days if he can't drive."

"Oh!" was all John could think to say. He knew he had kept putting off having lessons, but Reg's action had certainly caught him unawares. He spent the rest of the afternoon deep in thought on the subject of driving, feeling a little apprehensive but, at the same time, looking forward to his first lesson. Looking even further into the future he began to compare the comforts of a car with the discomfort of a moped.

PIGEON AND RABBIT SHOOTING

John had usually taken his gun with him round his snares each morning, but had very little shooting so he was pleased when Reg suggested that they go pigeon shooting one afternoon. There were quite a number coming in to feed on a stubble and the thought of a chance of some proper shooting quite excited John. They had an enjoyable afternoon hidden in hides built in the hedge. Reg had cut a few branches to make himself and John a hide each and then he had carefully spread his plastic decoys out in front of the hides. They certainly fooled the pigeons into thinking that their mates had found some good feeding for they came swooping into land beside the decoys, after having flown over first and spied out the ground. Reg, as soon as he had killed a few, laid them out alongside the decoys so that they looked as though they were feeding, and after an hour Reg had quite a flock to lure the other pigeons within shooting range.

The following evening Reg had arranged to go night shooting rabbits with Fred at Stonelands so John enjoyed another sport that evening. Half an hour after it was dark Fred pulled in the yard with his four-wheel-drive pick up. They loaded a straw bale in the back along with a good supply of cartridges and two torches. Reg climbed into the back with his gun and John got in beside Fred who was driving, and so they set off. John had never been night shooting before although he had often heard people talking about it.

They drove up the track and turned in the first field. Fred zig-zagged his way a few yards out from the hedge and the field erupted with rabbits. Their eyes shone in the lights as they waited uncertain of what to do, some ran into the hedge, white tails flashing; others crouched low, transfixed by the powerful head lights. Reg shot a left and a right, the nearest one to the hedge he took first and then swung onto the other as it started to scamper towards safety. They tumbled over as the shots hit them and were dead when John picked them up. Fred continued round the field and criss-crossed it when he had completed the circuit. Reg shot eight altogether, one of which John had to chase after as it attempted to drag itself to the ditch. John caught it and hurriedly killed it before it could scream a warning to the others. He threw it in the back of the truck and quickly jumped back inside. The whole

Figure 9.4 Pigeon Decoys in Position

operation was performed as quickly and quietly as possible. Sometimes Reg would spot a rabbit before either Fred or John had seen it and he would tap on the roof so that they would swing the lights back to where it was.

John enjoyed himself, but his eyes soon ached with the concentration needed to distinguish rabbits as they crouched in the grass and several times he had thought he had spotted one only to discover it was a dock leaf or a mole hill. Occasionally a bird would suddenly rise from the ground or a mouse would be seen scuttling away. Moths would appear in the lights and it seemed that nature was every bit as busy at night as she was during the day. Fred thought he had seen a fox in one field and he accelerated after it. John held on tight and wondered how Reg was feeling in the back as they hurtled across the field only to discover it was a deer. Reg was a good shot and missed very few rabbits. John marvelled how ever he could aim straight as he was bumped around in the back, but aim straight he did and there were not many escaped that he fired at.

They drove round the last field that they could go in and John looked at his watch as he picked the last rabbit — it was eleven thirty — how quickly the time had passed. They pulled up outside the shed that served as a game larder and set about unloading and hanging up the rabbits.

John carried them in, Reg made a small slit above the hock on one hind leg and pushed the other leg through it so that the legs were crossed. Fred braced them up along the rail back to back by hooking one rabbit's legs over anothers. Soon they were all hung neatly along the rail, head downwards and Reg counted up. The total was sixty, a good evening's work that should please the farm manager.

John felt uncomfortable — he had rabbits' hairs tickling his nose, his hands were sticky with blood and the little black fleas crawling on the rabbits ears made him want to scratch. He was glad that Reg asked him in for a cup of coffee and made to wash his hands as soon as he went into the kitchen. The clock on the mantlepiece struck midnight as Reg poured out the coffee and John declined the offer of a tot of whiskey in it to warm him up. Reg had got quite cold sitting in the open back of the truck, but John and Fred had been warm enough in the front.

John sat back in the armchair and listened as the men discussed the evening's work; they progressed on to other rabbiting expeditions both night shooting and ferreting. John excused himself after half an hour, the warmth of the kitchen and tiredness combined to make staying awake an impossibility.

DRIVING LESSONS COMMENCE

The following Wednesday afternoon saw John nervously waiting by the gate for the driving instructor to arrive. Reg had warned him to forget anything he thought he may have learned in the landrover, so later when the instructor enquired whether he had driven before he answered no.

The instructor drove along the lane until he came to a place that was straight and level. He stopped, turned off the engine and carefully explained the mechanics of driving and then asked John how much he knew of the highway code, something which John had already made himself familiar with.

The instructor got out and John slid himself across into the driver's seat — it did feel peculiar after the landrover, the plush comfort of the seats, the light steering wheel and the assortment of dials. Despite following the instructions, John's first attempt at pulling away was uncomfortably jerky and his second attempt somewhat noisy as he raced the engine. Nevertheless, the hour soon passed and John arranged to have an hour's lesson each week.

ACTIVITIES CONTINUE

Sally's lessons continued every evening and John had advanced to teaching her to stop when she was away from him. He found this quite hard, but eventually could stop her when she was on the way out to get the dummy although he found this difficult to perfect. Sometimes he would call her back to him and other times he would send her on for the dummy giving her the command 'back'. He also started to teach her hand signals by throwing dummies either side of her and waving his arm in whichever direction he wished her to go. At first she would sometimes go for the wrong one and he would quickly blow the stop whistle and walk out to her to put her back where she was to start with. He also spent some time each lesson throwing out dummies and making her watch while he fetched them himself — instilling into her mind that she was not required to pick everything that fell and curbing her natural instinct to retrieve anything she had seen fall. This lesson was perhaps the most important for steadiness was the most vital factor when working a dog in a line of beaters. John made sure, as well, that he never gave her very long retrieves because when working in line she must stay near to him all the time, never being more than a few yards away when she was hunting.

The month of September was drawing to an end and the new shooting season would soon be here, although at Stonelands it would be the beginning of November before they started shooting. They had another night out rabbit shooting with Fred and they shot nearly as many as the first night they had been out.

Reg told John that he had better have a long weekend at home before the end of the month as there would be no chance of a day off once they started feeding out. Reg promised faithfully to look after John's pen and Sally while he was away and was gratified to see the lad was still in two minds about going. He would like to see his brothers and parents again, but loathe to leave his pheasants and pup. Finally he decided to go home Friday afternoon and come back Monday morning and it amused Reg that John spent the entire journey to the station instructing him on looking after the pheasants and Sally. It pleased him to know that John had got so involved with his job.

He watched the lad as he bought his ticket at the station and waved as he went through to the platform. What a difference his parents would notice in him; he had altered a lot from the shy gangling youth he had picked up at the station six months previously. He had filled out, and although still shy with strangers he had grown confident with Reg although in no way big headed. Moreover, he could be trusted too and Reg was glad he had chosen John from the numerous applicants for the job. Mind you, he still had a lot to learn, but he was well on the way to making a good keeper and he was still as keen to learn as when he arrived. Never too old to learn thought Reg as he got back into the landrover — even I am still doing that and I've been keepering nearly thirty years.

Figure 9.5
The Majestic Pheasant

Counting and
Planning
10

OCTOBER

Figure 10.1   A Brown Hare Relaxes   **courtesy photo: Robin Williams**

COUNTING AND PLANNING

As John left the caravan the rain lashed down, he was hot inside his waterproofs, but glad of them all the same. The spell of fine weather ended with September and soon everywhere was wet and muddy. John was embarking on a new routine that would continue more or less all through the Winter. Reg had bought some new feed bags during the Summer and from now on they would be used daily to carry corn round the woods from the feed bins. John's mornings now were spent with feeding his pen before breakfast and then afterwards he checked his snares and traps and fed the outlying woods and covers, with only a slight variation to take in the Birches and the farthest end of the kale that the cows had now started. The route he followed was the same as earlier in the year when he had first arrived.

SHOOT PREPARATIONS

The afternoons he and Reg spent either taking corn round to the feed bins in the landrover or trimming out tracks that would be needed later on for sewelling and for gun stands. They also cut gun sticks so that the numbers could be wedged in the top to show the guns where they should stand for each drive.

Reg suggested while they were having dinner that as it was still raining they might as well make up some more sewelling that afternoon and so they got themselves organised with plastic, artificial bags and a large ball of plastic baler twine. Reg instructed John to roll the bags up and cut them into two inch wide segments. Reg unwound each segment and knotted it to the string which he had hung to and fro across the shed. John thought it looked like ribbons. Reg showed him how to gather it up and carefully tie it when they had finished, for if it was put away correctly it would be easy to play out along the track where it was required to stop the pheasants from running over.

The rain cleared away later in the afternoon prompting Reg to suggest that they had a drive round in the landrover.

"Now's the time to see what pheasants we've got," he said, "they'll all be out drying off after this rain."

He took the landrover along the fields that had not yet been cultivated and John was surprised to see so many pheasants. When he walked round in the mornings he had not been seeing very many, and they had not started to feed properly on the freshly cut tracks, but now they showed. Reg drove round his own beat as well as John's and afterwards announced that he was satisfied with what he had seen. John, besides being glad to see the pheasants on his own beat had enjoyed the opportunity to have a look round Reg's; apart from taking the poults to the release pens and filling the corn bins he had not had much chance to look round and he intended to have an afternoon or two walking round, for the last thing he wanted to happen on a shoot day was for him to lose himself.

THE PHEASANTS ARE MATURING

The pheasants, apart from the youngest ones of all were very nearly full grown; an odd cock bird still displayed a pale stripe of juvenile feathers down his breast and a few looked spikey around their heads where the new feathers were not yet fully grown, but in the main it was hard to tell the young pheasants from the mature ones.

John still fed his pheasants at his pen in the evenings as well as the mornings, and had been worrying as the number feeding was slowly dwindling. Reg had not seemed unduly concerned the evening when he had driven up to see how John was doing. He knew from experience that besides feeding out round the woods the birds were finding an abundance of natural feed. The blackberries that still flourished in the hedges, as well as acorns and beech masts were providing a greater attraction than the wheat on offer at the pen.

There was still some stubble left and insects still abounded, in fact Reg had watched his own poults a few days earlier as they had chased daddy-long-legs through the grass. Every year as it neared the first shoot day the birds would go off feeding, and every year he worried a little, but an odd afternoon after several hours rain they would show and allay his fears. Reg tried to teach the lad the skill that was needed in feeding the pheasants, judging the necessary amount needed to keep the birds hungry enough to come regularly at feed times while not making them so hungry that they looked elsewhere for food. Reg believed that feeding was probably one of the most important skills that contributed to being a good keeper and if he could teach John how to feed correctly he would be very satisfied.

TRAINING SALLY THE DOG

Unknown to John, Reg had been keeping a watchful eye on his progress with Sally and he was surprised one lunchtime when Reg suggested that he should take Sally round feeding with him in the mornings.

"I think she is obedient enough for you to take her", Reg had said. "It will give her a chance to get used to game and the exercise will get her fit — always make sure you've got a bit of string in your pocket though in case she misbehaves, for you don't want her frightening your pheasants away!"

The first morning John had taken her he had not trusted her much, saying 'no' every time she turned to look at a rabbit or a pheasant. He had left her on 'stay' at one or two places, but he kept creeping back to see if she was still there. She had looked at him as much as to say 'what's the matter — what do you keep coming back for', but he couldn't believe she would remember her training now she was in a fresh place and with temptation surrounding her. She did remember her training and as the days passed John's confidence and trust in her grew so that he no longer worried that she would not stay where she was left or would leave his heel. The only thing he did have problems with was cows — she hated them and if he needed to cross the field they were in he had to put her on the string and very nearly drag her along. She would tuck her tail between her legs and hang her head low occasionally glancing pathetically up at John so that he felt quite guilty at betraying her trust in him.

POSSIBLE POACHERS

One evening John noticed a blue van driving slowly along the lane and he thought little of it until he saw it again a day or two later. He mentioned it to Reg the following morning and was surprised when Reg said that Fred had seen it cruising along his roads as well. Later, at dinner time the phone had rung while they were eating their dinner. Reg answered it and when he returned he told John that it was Fred ringing about the van. Apparently it was two gypsies or pikies as Reg called them who were driving round in the evenings shooting pheasants. The passenger had a powerful air rifle and he would shoot at the pheasants out of the window. Reg had discovered in the past that the best deterrent to this was to drive round the roads in his landrover making his presence obvious; he suggest that John should have a look round on his moped but warned him:

"Don't tackle them if you see them, they can be quite nasty — just make sure you get their number. If they think they've been seen sometimes they'll leave the place alone."

ANTICIPATION AND PREPARATION

John was beginning to look forward to the first shoot. A few frosts had changed the leaves from green to the yellows and golds of Autumn. The trees were a blaze of colour in the Autumn sunshine and the wind showered the leaves down and bundled them into heaps in corners and gateways.

Reg came back from shopping one afternoon and called John over to the house, holding out a large carrier bag he said.

"Present for you — on the firm."

John took the bag and looked inside — in it was a new Barbour coat and waterproof trousers.

"Thanks", he said, knowing how expensive these items were.

"One year the guv'nor provides me with a suit and the other year I have waterproofs. This year it's the waterproofs. You should by rights have a suit, but as you are still growing perhaps it's just as well it's waterproofs this year — all being well you will have a proper suit next year", Reg told him.

"That's all right", answered John slightly disappointed that he didn't have a suit, but at the same time seeing the sense of what Reg said.

"By the way", Reg continued, "You'd better get your hair cut before next month. I can't abide sloppy looks and sloppy manners, and you'll have to wear a hat and a tie."

"I've got both", replied John grinning to himself as he remembered Roger's predictions. "I bought a hat at the Game Fair and my mum and dad gave me a tie with pheasants on it for my birthday."

"Good — as I said you'll have a suit like mine next year all being well", Reg told him again sensing the lad's disappointment over the suit.

John felt some comfort from the last remark as it meant that Reg was including him in next season's plans. At least it did not sound as though he was thinking of sacking him at the end of the present season.

John was pleased when the clocks were altered, although the evenings were long and he needed to feed his pen before tea in the afternoons; he found it much nicer to have it lighter in the mornings. Several times when it had been cloudy he found himself waiting for the birds to come off roost before he could feed them. He preferred to leave them a little while after they came down as they seemed rather stupid at first, almost as if they needed a quarter of an hour before they were properly awake. They were however beginning to feed a little better as the weather grew colder and the days shorter.

He enjoyed feeding round each morning for although he took the same route every day there was always something interesting to see. Sometimes it was an unusual bird or sometimes he would catch a glimpse of a shrew or a vole common enough, but seldom seen. One morning he watched as a cow calved in the corner of a field. It was showing the calf's head and front legs when he first saw it and he watched with interest as the calf completed its arrival and the cow got up and turned straight round to lick it, her rough tongue removing the membranes and continuing to massage it. John was worried because the calf lay still for a few moments, but suddenly it raised its wet head, its ears flopping loosely and it snorted as it took its first breath.

John watched as the cow carried on licking as it struggled. He knew he was wasting time so he continued on his way. When he crossed the other side of the field a while later he could see that already the calf was on its feet suckling.

Another morning he had heard a commotion in the dry leaves under a beech tree; at first he thought it was two cocks fighting but as he crept closer he could see that it was a stoat and a squirrel fighting. He stood still and watched for what seemed an age as the two animals were locked in combat wishing that he had not left his gun at home, but at the same time fascinated as to what the outcome would be. The stoat, a ferocious little animal that frequently killed rabbits three times its size had met its match with the squirrel armed as it was with sharp teeth and claws. Twice the stoat lost its hold of the squirrel and it broke free, but instead of running to safety up the trunk of the tree it ran around it on the ground until the stoat seized hold of it again. Some sudden noise or scent suddenly caused the squirrel and the stoat to part, the squirrel disappeared down a rabbit hole and the stoat into a tree root. John spent the rest of the day puzzling why the squirrel had not climbed to safety up the tree trunk when it had the chance — was it stupidity or fright that had made it behave so.

John found the evenings tedious at first, but he soon came to terms with the possible boredom. He arranged to have his weekly driving lesson in the evenings. Occasionally he would go out with Roger and he borrowed some books from Reg about old time keepers and poachers. John eagerly read through these thinking that the old men would turn in their graves if they could see the modern ways. Long gone were the days where an estate boasted a veritable array of keepers and rabbit catchers, when rearing was all done with broody hens and the food all carefully cooked for the chicks. John thought that the pheasants on the estate probably lived better than the farm worker. Poaching too seemed to be a profession spiced with the added excitement of trying to outwit the keeper.

He discovered that there were programmes on the television which he could now watch regularly. Throughout the Summer there had been very little time to watch the television and he had completely lost touch with some of the series.

Reg and Fred had started on their nightly patrols, mostly having a look round together some time during the evening accompanied by Fred's German Shepherd Dog*, Sabre. John had been told that he would have to take a turn with one or other of them some nights and he quite looked forward to the excitement, Reg had quickly warned him that there was nothing very exciting about being out in a draughty landrover on a freezing

***In fact, Fred called his dog an Alsation now renamed a German Shepherd dog by the Kennel Club.**

Figure 10.2   Dreaming of Old Time Keeping

cold night, waiting for something that might not happen. The blue van had not been seen in the vicinity for several days and Reg hoped that they would have no more bother from the diddicoys.

John no longer took his gun with him round his snares. Reg made a rule that neither would carry a gun during the shooting season so that if they heard a shot it should be investigated.

Most mornings John took Sally with him. The pheasants had soon got used to her and ignored her presence, she in turn took little notice of them except if one came really close then she would watch it intently.

John plucked up courage one day and asked Reg if he might take her shooting. He thought for a moment before answering.

"I don't really see why not, but you'll have to keep her to heel all day and you must be certain she'll behave. I can't abide wild dogs."

John had been very strict with Sally and he was as certain as he could be that she would do as she was told; he had always made sure that she had obeyed his orders. He had thrown so many dummies out which he had fetched himself ensuring she would be perfectly steady that he was convinced he got more exercise on the training sessions than the dog did.

He knew it would be impossible to beat through the cover if he had her on a lead. This would be continually getting caught up so he would have to trust her off it; he knew there was only one way he could find out how she would behave on a shoot day – and that was to take her.

John had spent two Sunday afternoons walking around Reg's beat, familiarising himself with the woods and hedges; Reg called it doing his homework and he was pleased that the lad had taken enough interest to bother in his own time. In Reg's opinion all these little things added up to the making of a good keeper and if Reg had any doubts about John's interest in the job or being trustworthy he would have little hesitation in looking for a replacement the following season. Reg's job like that of most keepers was somewhat dependent on results and his under-keeper was partly responsible for those results so for Reg it was vital to have someone he could trust implicitly working with him.

The Final Inspection

The last few days of October were very busy days for John and Reg. Mr. Brinklow and Reg went round the drives that were planned for the first days shoot and stuck in the gun sticks where the nine guns who would be shooting were to stand. Together with Mr. Brinklow the eight other men

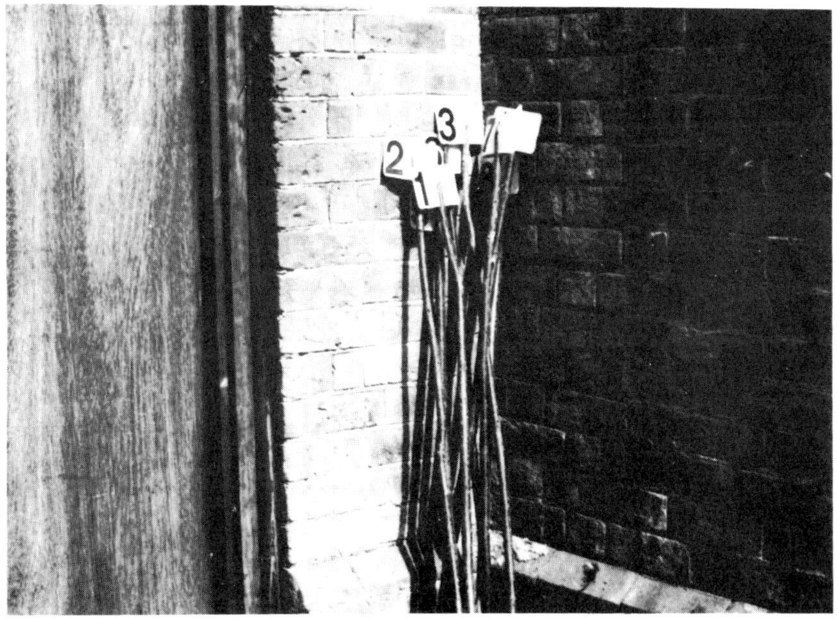

Figure 10.3   Gun Stands (Sticks or Pegs)

paid a subscription to cover the cost of the shoot. The expenses were far too great for Mr. Brinklow alone with the cost of rearing the pheasants, wages, the landrover and other day-to-day running costs so to enable him to enjoy shooting on his own estate he had formed a syndicate, some of whom had been shooting at Stonelands for as long as Reg could remember. To give everyone an equal chance of a good day's shooting the numbers were drawn at the beginning of a shoot day and by moving up two places for each drive no-one was left at the same number peg for every drive. Mr. Brinklow, although he knew where every gun stood for every drive, continued each year to walk round with Reg when it came time to put the gun sticks out. The two men had set up a very good working relationship over the years, Reg leaving the responsibility of organising the guns entirely to Mr. Brinklow who in turn never interfered with the way Reg handled the beaters and the pickers-up. The pre-shoot walk round gave the two of them a chance to discuss the forthcoming shoot so that there would be no confusion on the actual day. A well organised day added a lot the enjoyment of all concerned. While the boss and the head keeper went out John was left to tidy up one of the sheds and fetch some straw bales in for the beaters to sit on when they stopped for lunch; he also rigged up an old gas heater to a partly filled cylinder of gas that was left from the rearing season — it might help to warm the shed through on a cold day.

John had seen very little of Mr. Brinklow for he seldom bothered Reg; occasionally he would take a look round but more often than not if Reg wanted to see him he had to call up the big house. Reg sometimes cursed at having to waste time going in search of Mr. Brinklow when he needed to see him, but all in all it was far preferential to having a boss who was always calling round and interfering.

BEATING

John had been allowed to go out beating one day as well. It was only a small shoot on the boundary but the keeper who cared for it never missed a day at Stonelands so Reg thought it was only fair that one of them should go to help him out. Reg always went picking up on Fred's estate and in turn Fred picked up at Stonelands. John enjoyed his day out but being on a Monday he had to spend nearly all day feeding on the Sunday. He had fed as usual in the morning and after he had done his pen in the afternoon he fed the places he knew he would not have time to do next morning. The food would then at least be there for the birds the following day even if it wasn't delivered at the usual time. He only left himself two places to feed in the morning besides his pen because he knew that time would be short.

The keeper on the other shoot wanted him there by quarter past nine and it would take him ten minutes on his moped. The day had been spent shooting the outlying hedgerows and woods and as they only released a few hundred the bag was not very large at the end of the day. The boss was a jovial fellow and seemed quite happy to go out and only shoot a few pheasants, but John knew that Reg would have little interest in a shoot that was ran in such a light hearted way.

DETAILED INSTRUCTIONS ARE GIVEN

Later in the week prior to their first shoot Reg and John had taken two bundles of sewelling and placed them where they would be needed on the day. They drove on round the rest of the planned drives and Reg explained carefully how each drive was done and what he would expect of John. He wanted him to be completely familiar with the drives and to know which order they were going to be done. Eight were planned, three in the afternoon and five in the morning and Reg emphasised to John that he would much prefer him to ask any questions now than bother him unnecessarily on the shoot day.

There was little time the preceding day to do much except feeding. Reg went off to make the final arrangements with Martin and Arthur the two tractor drivers on the estate, who offered their services on a shoot day. One drove the game cart and the other the beaters' trailer each using his own tractor. They had been coming for years and knew exactly what Reg required of them. Such help was invaluable on a busy day and Reg was very grateful to have such people as part of the team. While Reg was gone John washed the landrover feeling a certain satisfaction as he washed away the dirt and hosed off great lumps of mud from the wheel arches. He swept out the front and pulled out some dirt from beside the seat where some wheat that had been dropped had taken root and was growing a couple of inches high. He stood back when he had finished and admired his handiwork for it looked almost as though it was new except for the dents.

Reg came hurrying towards him!

"I've just remembered that I have forgotten to cut some strings if you know what I mean", he said, "I'll show how I do it and then if you ever get five minutes spare you can get some done."

Reg went to the shed and sorted through a large box underneath the table. He pulled out a board with two nails stuck in and placed it on the table. He reached for the ball of binder twine at the back and proceeded to wind it round the nails.

"There you are — count out twenty five and then cut through the strings. You will then have twenty five pieces all the right length for bracing the birds together. Take one length out — knot the ends together and loop it round the other strings like this so it holds them together", Reg showed him. "When it comes to tying the birds up you pull out a bit of string, knot the ends together, loop one end round the pheasants neck and pull it tight, then make a loop in the other end and put it over the second pheasants head — always brace a cock and a hen together, if possible, and then hang them up as soon as you can."

Reg demonstrated to John how it was done and then quickly cut another two bundles.

"That should be more than enough for tomorrow; we usually get about a hundred on each of the first two days — I wonder what else I might have forgotten. It's the same every year, once we've started shooting it all falls into a routine, but to start with it's easy to overlook something. I'll go and hang these up ready in the game cart." — Reg told John and he turned and walked away mumbling about having done the beaters' money and having seen Ned and Bert about stopping and what else .....

John set off to feed his pen that afternoon full of excitement. It would be another three weeks before this was shot, but tomorrow they would be doing the Birches and Reg had instructed him not to feed the wood. John had not been seeing very many birds there, but it was near the boundary and Reg had not seemed very concerned when John told him how many he usually fed. When he had done his pen he set off to feed the rest of the places for he knew there would be little time to spare in the morning. It was nearly dark by the time he reached the last wood and all round him the pheasants

Figure 10.4 Sewelling

were going to roost. Some evenings he had sat down in different woods and counted them as they flew up into the branches; they would walk quietly into the wood and then peer about as if selecting a suitable branch. The cock birds would fly up with a noisy chatter and call to one another; the hens did not make so much noise usually only uttering a single tweet as they flew up. Every night the woods were noisy with their bed time preparations.

John got back to the caravan and fed Sally, talking to her as she greedily ate, reminding her not to forget her training and begging her to behave herself. She wagged her tail and licked his face.

He got his own tea when he had tended to his dog's needs and then settled down to watch the television but his thoughts were on the day to come and he could not concentrate on watching.

He went to bed early as he wanted to be up punctual, but he knew sleep would not come easy for his mind reeled with Reg's instructions and thoughts of Sally on her first shoot day. His thoughts turned into nightmares as his brain galloped on envisaging all the things that could go wrong. He felt tired but his brain would not stop — if only he could turn it off.

Reg too had a restless night, his mind full of the following day's shooting. Despite his years of experience he was still unable to feel relaxed about a day's shooting especially the first one of every season. Not until Christmas time when the big days were over would he cease to worry so much over each day — by then he would know whether the season was a good one or a poor one. His brain mulled over the details of the morrow. He had put the sewelling where old Ben would know where to find it for it was his job to hang it up where it was needed and pull it if the birds tried to run underneath. His mind turned to the stops; Ned and Bert would be waiting for him at first light for it was their job to keep the pheasants in one of the woods on the boundary. It was only a small field away from the neighbour's ground and without the stops there the birds might well stray away during the day only returning to the wood to roost in the evening. Ned and Bert knew their job and he could trust them not to let any pheasants stray off. Fred would be in charge of the pickers up so Reg had no worries about them. Reassuring himself that all the necessary people had been contacted and that he had taken care of the sewelling, the stops and beaters' money and beer his thoughts turned to John. How would the lad behave and was he right allowing him to take the pup. Both John and Sally seemed quite sensible and Reg hoped that his judgement had been wise — only time would tell.

Eventually sleep came to both Reg and John and a full moon shone out of the clear cold sky.

Figure 10.5   A Shooting Party at Wilton Long Ago

The Shooting Season Begins
11

NOVEMBER

Figure 11.1   Rabbits Coming Out to Feed   **courtesy photo: Pamela Harrison**

THE SHOOTING SEASON BEGINS

MONTH: **NOVEMBER**

AN EARLY START

Reg woke before the alarm rang, it was still dark and he dressed quietly trying not to disturb his wife, but she, as usual, also woke. "Don't worry — I'll get my own breakfast, you stay there and I'll bring you a cup of tea up", Reg told her as he sat on the bed and pulled on his socks.

He was pouring the tea out when he saw the light in the caravan go on — he was pleased the lad had got up early and allowed himself plenty of time for lateness and untidiness were foreign to Reg's nature.

John had just finished his breakfast when he saw Reg leave in his landrover to pick up Ned and Bert. John looked outside. He guessed that it was cold and the grass was crisp. The sky in the East was beginning to lighten; at last the shooting season had arrived at Stonelands.

The pheasants were still swooping down out of the trees to land in the ride when John reached his pen; they stood as though collecting their wits about them before coming up to feed. He threw out the corn along the ride and then walked quickly back to the caravan. He hastily changed into a clean shirt and some brown cords. Then he fumbled about trying to tie his tie correctly — he could not remember when he had last worn one and it took three attempts before he could get the knot in the right place. The sun shone warmly into the caravan making him decide on a thin jumper underneath his Barbour coat. The butterflies that had fluttered in his stomach earlier had quietened down as the day progressed. He had little time to feel nervous being more pre-occupied with the problem of presenting a smart appearance. He quickly drank a mug of coffee and stuffed a packet of biscuits in his pocket; he cut himself a slice of cake and ate it, breakfast already seemed an age distant. He searched in the cupboard for his hat and had just found it when Reg tapped on the door.

THE DOGS ARE EXERCISED

"Good, I'm glad you're ready — can you give the dogs a run in the field and let them empty themselves — I'll take Honey and Amber. I'm just going to get changed", he shouted.

John opened the kennel gates and called the dogs, as he walked across the orchard. They barked and jumped about unusually excited, even Jet's stiff old legs had miraculously loosened up so she too frisked about and she was very unwilling to be shut back in her kennel. John went back to the caravan to fetch Sally's whistle that he had nearly forgotten and then walked over to the shed to sort out the thumb stick he had cut for himself one afternoon when he had been trimming out the feed rides. He fetched a lead out of his coat pocket and put Sally on it and then went over to wait by the landrover.

Reg came out of the house and then disappeared back in for a moment.

"Nearly forgot my whistles — have you got yours?" he explained as he re-emerged from the house and walked over to the vehicle. His dogs milled around his feet, tails wagging and panting with excitement making it difficult to unfasten the tail gate and lower it so that they could jump in. Eventually they and Sally were safely installed and Reg climbed into the driver's seat.

"Anyone would think that your dogs knew they were going shooting", John told him. "They were excited as soon as I let them out of the kennel even old Jet."

"Aye — they know all right — they were sitting by the gates when I went out first thing. Any other morning they would have still been curled up in the straw — it's uncanny how they know. I had my ordinary work clothes on earlier so it wasn't seeing me in my suit that gave them a clue", Reg answered. As he spoke Jet started howling her mournful indignation at being left behind.

"Poor old girl — her spirit is still willing but her body's too weak — I sometimes think it would be kinder to put her down than have to leave her behind each shoot day — it's a pity they don't live longer", Reg said sadly, remembering her as a puppy as if it were only yesterday.

ASSEMBLY AT STONELANDS

Reg pulled into the stable yard at the back of the big house at one minute to nine. Mr. Brinklow came out and bid them each good morning — no other guns had yet arrived as they met at nine fifteen. He exchanged a few words with Reg before the sound of a car pulling up on the gravelled drive in front of the house caused him to turn and he walked through the archway to shake hands with the first arrival.

John sat in the landrover and watched as a variety of cars came down the drive and pulled into the stable yard. By twenty past nine there was an assortment of old and new cars, push bikes and motor bikes, two landrovers and Fred's pick-up parked untidily round the yard. Fred had a smart fibre glass back fitted to his pick-up truck and inside John could see his two black labradors peering through the back window. Reg had left John in the landrover while he had chatted to the beaters, but he came back and fetched John in order to take him round to the front of the house and introduce him to the guns.

"Don't forget to take your hat off and shake hands", Reg said gruffly making John suddenly feel shy.

They walked through the archway and the drive in front of the house was a hive of activity. Parked around the drive were two Range Rovers, a landrover, a sports car, two expensive looking saloon cars, two small hatch backs and a Rolls Royce. An assortment of men, women and dogs were swarming about unloading wellingtons, coats, shooting sticks, guns and cartridges from within the vehicles. John smiled at the scene that presented itself; two of the women looked as though they had stepped from the pages of a glossy magazine. The men were dressed in tweeds. The dogs were busy getting in everyone's way. There were two black labradors, one yellow one, an ancient golden retriever and a very active spaniel that added to the confusion by upsetting one of the labradors. A snarl of anger and a flash of teeth caused a vociferous response from both owners; the dogs parted, but for several minutes afterwards the labrador could be seen strutting around stiff legged with 'hackles' raised and cocking its leg on any available object, including the shooting stick that a red-faced colonel was resting his excessive weight upon.

Mr. Brinklow called out and some semblance of order was rendered from the apparent chaos as they gathered around him.

Introductions

"This is our new under-keeper, John", said Mr. Brinklow who then proceeded to introduce each gun to John. With the introductions over the guns drew for their numbers for the first drive, after that they would move up two places for each drive.

Reg and John walked back through the archway; Arthur and Martin had arrived with the beaters' trailer and the game cart so Reg got the beaters organized while John let the dogs out of the landrover. They quivered with excitement, Honey and Amber leaped straight up on the trailer and sat amongst the beaters on the straw bales. John kept Sally on the lead and here he encountered his first problem — she would not jump up on the trailer — so he hastily lifted her up and clambered up himself, Sally then tried to climb onto Roger's lap and lick his face which he didn't appreciate. John sat

Figure 11.2   Assembly Before the Shoot

down and looked round the faces on the trailer — he only knew a few. Reg quickly told them all John's name and then shouted to Arthur to move off.

THE SHOOT BEGINS

John took another look around as they bumped along the track. The beaters came in a variety of sizes and shapes and clothing, each had a stick, some already bearing signs of previous usage. Their clothing was of a wide variety from anoraks to Barbours with a predominance of black P.V.C.; in fact, one old man was clothed entirely in it — his body encased in P.V.C. over-trousers and a long coat and a P.V.C. cap adorned his head. Nearly all the beaters wore wellingtons and leggings to protect them from the brambles or the wetness of the kale. The sun shone warm on John's back as he fondled Sally's ears and wondered if the old chap clad in P.V.C. was sweating inside of it.

Arthur stopped the tractor near the first wood and they all disembarked. Ned and Bert joined them and informed Reg that to their knowledge they had not let any birds pass them. John saw the dying embers of a fire alongside the hedge and he could smell whisky on Ned's breath. He drew the conclusion that the early morning frost had not bothered the two old men unduly.

The beaters spread themselves out along the width of the first wood and waited for Mr. Brinklow to blow his whistle to inform Reg that all was ready. Reg answered the signal with two blasts on his own whistle and they started the first drive.

The morning passed quickly. John had let Sally off the lead as soon as he sensed she was a little calmer, but he kept her strictly to heel and put her back on the lead whenever she was near to several people. It seemed to be people that confused her more than anything and she seemed to soon lose John when there were a number of people around to distract her. She took little notice of the pheasants as they flew up having got used to them already. Several beaters had chatted to John during the morning and he began to feel less of an outsider. They reached the Birches just before lunch and John was pleased to hear that the guns shot eighteen out of it. From where he was they appeared to miss several as well and he certainly had not been seeing that number there when he fed.

Reg seemed satisfied with the morning's bag of sixty seven and even asked John how Sally had behaved. They found a spare bale of straw to sit on in the shed and Reg handed John a can of beer and some sandwiches. Mrs. Plummer brought them all out a large pan of hot soup and the beaters quickly queued up for a mug full each.

The pickers up arrived at the shed in time to share the soup and were grateful that Reg had saved them some beer. John had only seen them in the distance during the morning and had yet to meet two of them. Fred, of course, he knew; there was Ernie who had two labradors and a spaniel and Hazel — a woman in her thirties who had two golden retrievers. They discussed the morning's shooting with Reg and apologiséd for not being able to find a runner from the last drive. They had all spent several minutes searching for it to no avail and had even wondered that it might have been wishful thinking by the gun to say that he had hit it.

Reg finished his sandwiches and withdrew a parcel of envelopes from his pocket. He handed round the pay and told the men that as soon as they were finished he would make a move as there was a plantation to blank in to the drive proper before the guns arrived. John decided to leave Sally at home during the afternoon; she had behaved fairly well, but she had curled up at his feet coming back on the trailer at lunch time and he thought she felt tired — a morning was plenty for her to start with and together they had walked several miles. Honey and Amber did not seem the least bit tired when Reg let them back out of the kennel despite having worked hard pushing through the cover to rout the pheasants. John had watched them work and admired the way they stayed near to Reg working individually and missing nothing; he had seen Honey wind a bird several yards away and work her way along the scent almost as if she could see it. When Amber scented a bird sitting tight under the brambles; she would stand rigid and point at it giving the beaters time to rattle the bird out of the cover with their sticks.

Within a few minutes everyone was on the trailer. As they passed the big house John could see the guns back at their cars, and once again the guests were donning wellington boots and coats, chatting amongst themselves and smoking large cigars.

The afternoon passed even quicker than the morning and the sun was a fiery red ball in the sky when Reg blew the final whistle to indicate the end of the last drive. The air was chilly as the beaters clambered on the trailer for the last time that day. Arthur drove them back to the big house and they climbed off and were soon away in their cars and on their bikes leaving Reg and John alone in the once-again peaceful stable yard. Fred drove his truck in beside them and the three pickers up and their seven dogs got out. Martin drove in with the game cart and again the stable yard was no longer quiet. Reg sorted out nine good brace of pheasants — one for each of the guns who had been shooting and checked with Martin that the day's total was one hundred and seventeen. He then asked John to help Martin hang the pheasants in the game larder at home and to take Honey and Amber back with him. Reg then disappeared through the archway carrying the nine brace.

Martin and John hung the pheasants up on the hooks; there were forty six brace hung round the shed. Besides the pheasants were three French

Figure 11.3 Pheasant Shooting: Beaters Walking through Kale   **courtesy photo: Roy Shaw**

partridges, three pigeons and a jay. Martin backed the game cart under the tractor shed alongside the rearing equipment and drove off down the lanes to his own house leaving John alone in the yard. It was too late to feed his pen for already he could hear the birds going to roost in the distance — he did not like missing them, but an odd night should not hurt. He shut Amber and Honey in their kennel and fetched their food from the shed. They quickly ate it and were soon curled up in the straw as was Sally in her kennel.

Some time later he heard the landrover pull into the yard and a few moments after a tap on his door. He answered it and Reg stood outside.

"I've got your share of the tips here — the guns seemed pleased with the day", he said handing John the notes. "Sally behaved all right didn't she? You can take her again next time if you want, but I think you were wise leaving her home after dinner, she's only young and soon gets tired", he continued.

"Yes — she was O.K. and I kept her to heel the whole time and she never even had a retrieve", John answered.

"Don't worry about that; you teach her to be steady first, but, if you want, take one of those pheasants and throw it out for her to pick in the morning — make her wait before you send her and don't worry if she doesn't find it easy to pick up at first — she'll soon learn, If she does it right the first time only give her the one retrieve, but if you have any bother don't try it more than three or four times and if she still won't, then leave it and see me — I don't think you'll have any bother though", Reg added.

"O.K. I'll do that", answered John.

"Don't pick one that's badly shot — you want a clean one to start with — I must go; I haven't had my tea yet and whatever you've just cooked is making me feel very hungry. I'll see you in the morning", Reg told him as he turned towards his house.

"Goodnight", John called after him.

John shut the door and turned the television on.

REFLECTIONS ON THE DAY

He sat in the chair his eyes watching the picture and his mind mulling over the day's shooting.

He had seen little of the actual shooting and even less of the pickers up. The only dogs he had really been able to see working were Reg's animals and he hoped that one day Sally would be as good as them. He had noticed that no guns or pickers up had allowed their dogs to run about during the drives. Reg was quite adamant that the dogs should be only allowed to pick up after the whistle had indicated the end of each drive, with perhaps the exception of a picker up who was working a long way back from the guns. John hoped he would have more opportunity to see the shooting for it

Figure 11.4　The Game Larder at the End of the Day　　courtesy photo: **Frank H. Meads**

seemed odd to see the pheasants get up and fly and not know what was happening. One cock that he had seen shot surprised him; being some way off the sound of the shot reached his ears after the bird had begun to fall — it certainly seemed peculiar to see the bird fall before hearing the shot. He had learned the names of a few of the beaters, especially those that Reg kept shouting at because they couldn't keep in line as they should.

John felt tired as he laid back in the chair enjoying the warmth from the fire; slowly his eyes closed and he missed his favourite Saturday night programme.

AN INTERLUDE

The following days passed quickly by. The weather changed so that Bonfire Night was very nearly washed out. John went with Roger to the village bonfire celebrations — most of which were carried on in the pub on the green. At first everyone had gathered round the bonfire despite the rain, but the damp wood was unwilling to burn and the fireworks seemed to lack sparkle and it was not long before the least dedicated of the group were enjoying the warmth of the big log fire in the public bar of the inn.

Twice John went round with Reg at night on the look out for poachers, but there was nobody about except a courting couple in a car. Reg got out of the landrover and shone his torch on the steamed up windows. John laughed at the mad scrabble that ensued and the few choice words that were directed at Reg as he got back in the landrover.

"If you came round with Fred and me some nights and saw what we saw sometimes it would complete your education", Reg told John laughingly as he drove off.

The weather was wet for several days and then it became colder. For nearly a week it was raw cold and foggy — days when it barely got light and John needed to go and feed his pen well before four o'clock.

The second shoot was two weeks after the first and was very similar to the first one. Several of the drives they did again, besides which they drove out Reg's pen on the tenanted farm where the oldest poults had been released. This helped boost the bags total to one hundred and twenty eight.

Reg had started going to Fred's place picking up each Wednesday and so John was left to feed his pens in the afternoon as Reg fed John's birds on the Mondays that he was out beating. He liked doing Reg's pens and the opportunity to have a change of scenery.

A letter had arrived to say that he was to go for a driving test the following February so he continued with his driving lesson each week.

All the while, however, the big day was looming ahead, drawing nearer and nearer. His feelings of tension increased, added to by the fact that there was so much to do and very little day light to get it done in. Mr. Brinklow and Reg had got the sticks put out a few days before, but there was still corn bins to be filled, sewelling to take out, strings to cut, the landrover to wash and a hundred and one other jobs. The rain had softened the clay and everywhere was wet and mucky making most jobs unpleasant. John had spent sometime pulling up his snares and putting the safety catches on his traps because it would not do to have a dog caught up in either.

Sally had behaved well enough on the second shoot day. Once again John had kept her to heel and only had her out for the morning, but even so Reg suggested that he should leave her at home on the main days. Reg knew that John would have enough to think about without the pup and he hoped he would soon take a little more responsibility with the beaters, making them get loaded up on the trailer after each drive (instead of standing around chatting) and making sure that they kept in line during the drives. John had already seen how cunningly the pheasants would run back through the line if there was the slightest gap left in it and already he had learned that it was easier to tell them off than have Reg keep telling him off. He soon noticed which beaters were usually the culprits and tried to keep an extra watch on them. He did not like telling them, but it was preferable to being told off himself.

Reg had seemed satisfied when John told him what numbers he was feeding in each drive, but, even so, John was already having bad dreams about beating through the drives and never seeing a single pheasant. He knew they had fed regularly for several weeks, but he still worried that something might go wrong — perhaps another dog would come or perhaps poachers.

THE BIG DAY APPROACHES

The night before the big day he slept badly. There had been no feeding to do other than his pen because the whole lot was to be shot. He felt a twinge of guilt when he fed his birds that evening; it was like the Last Supper. He was happy to see the number there, but secretly hoped they would not recognise him the next day as he pushed them out of the bushes with his stick forcing them to fly over the guns and risk their lives. He hoped too the survivors would forgive him and still come back to feed. Stupid he knew it was, for that was all his work was about, but still he felt as if he was about to betray them.

John was up early, relieved that the day had arrived at last — the climax to his months of hard work. He had little to do except take Sally out; it seemed strange not to feed his pen. Reg had asked him to leave at quarter past nine and feed the artichokes at White House Shaw and to wait there for the beaters to arrive so that there was sure to be a good drive to begin the day with. He ate a leisurely breakfast and then washed all the kennels out. The butterflies in his stomach were already fluttering, made worse by having nothing to occupy him. He continually checked his watch until at last it was time to leave. He filled his feed bag with corn and set off across the fields trying to walk normally, but finding himself hurrying as if to get it over with. By the time he reached his feed ride he was short of breath, his lips felt dry and his throat felt tight, it was several moments before he could achieve any resemblance to his usual whistle.

The birds began to appear out of the cover, scratching amongst the straw as they had every other day. Soon there were the usual number busily pecking up the grain and John breathed a sigh of relief — he looked at them dispassionately — relieved to see them there, but sorry they were to be shot, he remembered what he had heard Reg say to someone once — they were a crop to be harvested just as the pigs and lambs and cattle were sent for slaughter when they were big enough, except with the pheasant there was a chance to escape.

The Beaters Arrive

He turned and walked to the end of the shaw. It seemed an age before he saw the beaters walking towards him and the landrovers and Range Rovers take the guns to the far end of the drive. John kept wishing they would hurry, fearing that the pheasants would disappear before the whistle blew to start the drive. At last they heard it and Reg answered with two short blasts on his whistle, the line of beaters spread out and the first drive started.

The beaters progressed through the artichokes and the shaw in a straight line, their sticks tapping and using their eyes to spot any pheasants that had chosen to tuck up in the cover in preference to running ahead of them. A quick poke with the stick and the bird would run or fly out in front. The line neared the end of the drive and John was beginning to fear that the pheasants had indeed disappeared as only a few had got up and flown, but then all of a sudden with a clatter of wings about fifty rose in the air at once and spread out over the guns as they flew towards the pen. A barrage of shots greeted them and John could see three fall dead to the ground. He could not see all the guns, but hoped they had bagged more than the three he had seen fall.

A pause for re-loading

Reg halted the beaters, allowing the guns to reload before moving forward; once again several more birds burst from the cover and once again Reg halted the beaters. In front of him John could see pheasants running to and fro undecided where to go. One old cock got up and flew back low over the beaters heads, John cursed but Ned, next to him in the line said:

"I bet that old cock has been doing that for years; did you see the length of his tail, I expect he's got spurs to match."

After several more stops and starts they reached the end of the drive and climbed over the fence, Reg blew the whistle and walked over to John.

"Nice few birds there lad", he said. "I don't think they shot too well though. Can you get off with the beaters and get lined up to do the kale. I left a couple of stops out there to be on the safe side while we did this drive so call them in when you get there." Reg turned and strode over to Mr. Brinklow, his dogs obediently by his side.

John watched for a moment as the dogs were signalled into action and the 'guns'* themselves walked round picking up the pheasants that laid dead on the grass around them. He called to the beaters to come with him and they walked off through the gateway and across the field to the kale in the distance. Reg soon joined them and they watched as the guns drove across in their vehicles, disembarked and made their way to the pegs. At last they heard Mr. Brinklow's whistle and they started the second drive!

Action Once More

The kale was dripping wet, although it had not rained, the cloud was too thick for the sun to penetrate and the day was damp and cold. John was glad of the protection of his waterproofs; even after a few yards the water was dripping off them and without their protection he would have been soaked already. He enjoyed the drive because the birds flew steadily and he could see nearly all of the shooting. The pheasants climbed as they left the kale and headed back towards the pen; by the time they passed over head of the guns they were high and flying fast resulting in some spectacular shots and some spectacular misses as well! Nearing the end of the kale there were a couple of flushes of birds. Once again Reg stopped the line for a moment and John was able to watch the shooting. Soon the whistle blew and he had to quickly get the beaters moving on their way; this time they walked back to the trailer waiting to take them out to Smith's Wood for the third drive.

The next three drives went according to plan and once again John was grateful for the protection of his waterproofs, particularly in the Mount where brambles grew in profusion. The Wilderness was the last of the three drives and John was pleased with the number of birds that flew out. However, it had been difficult to know how many birds fed in there, because they would sit under the holly until he had passed and if he walked back along the ride they would dive back in the cover as soon as they heard or saw him. He had felt there were quite a number there, especially as the corn

*The term is used to describe those carrying the guns rather than 'shooters' or simi-
lar noun.

Figure 11.5 Sussex Shoot in the Rain **courtesy photo: John Tarlton**

went and the ride was well scratched each day, but, even so, he was relieved to see them fly out.

Collecting The Birds

"Come on John — give us a hand with the birds", shouted Reg at the end of the last drive, so, while the beaters made their way back across the field to the waiting trailer John hurried across towards the guns. He took the pheasants that they had collected into a pile and carried them over to the game cart where Martin was tying them into braces and hanging them on the rails. John set about bracing them together, a cock with a hen, and he handed them up to Martin to hang up. Reg walked over to them with another handful and as he did so Honey dived into a bramble bush and pulled out a cock pheasant. She returned to Reg carrying the indignant pheasant gently in her mouth, wagging her tail. Reg took the bird from her and holding it by its wings he hit it over the head with his stick. The bird was still fluttering when he dropped it to the ground beside the others.

"That one nearly got away with it", Reg said to John as he looked at the bird now laying still on the ground."It's been a good morning John; I told you not to worry", he continued and turning to Martin: "How many have we got so far?"

"That's one hundred and forty five now", answered Martin hanging up the last brace, "the pickers up aren't in yet and there's probably a few in the guns vehicles."

"Not bad", Reg replied, "I was hoping to have one hundred and fifty at lunch so we won't be far out despite the poor shooting. That old Colonel hasn't hardly hit a thing all morning."

"Aye, the shooting's not been anything special", Martin agreed.

Lunch Time Break

Reg turned to John; "Come on lad, we'd better grab some lunch, it's half past one already and we've got to move off at two."

They walked across the field to where Reg had left his landrover, Reg reminded John of the two afternoon drives. They were both more complicated than the morning drives had been; the first one, Home Copse, had to be swung round so that the beaters formed a half circle to push the birds out of the corner nearest the pen. The last drive was the Pen itself and the beaters had to drive it in two halves, bringing one half across and then lining out again to drive the birds out towards the guns.

Reg and John ate their sandwiches quickly when they got back. What soup was left was cold, but someone had put a can of beer aside for each of them for which they were glad. Reg was handing round the pay packets when the pickers up arrived in. They had been kept very busy all morning and Fred had missed one drive completely through staying behind at the previous drive to look for three runners. He had found two, but thought the third had gone into the Pen Wood and he knew better than to go near there. Including the pheasants they had brought in with them and those Martin had fetched from the Range Rovers the total was one hundred and sixty seven.

Reg was in a good mood as the beaters climbed back on the trailer while the pickers up ate their sandwiches; they would not need to move off until the guns were ready which would be another twenty minutes.

The Afternoon Session

The beaters were lined out and had been waiting for ten minutes before the guns arrived. The sky had grown darker but the rain had held off so far. Finally the whistle went and the line of beaters moved forward. Slowly Reg pushed the right hand beater forward until the line formed an arc across the corner of the wood. The pheasants started to rise and Reg moved first the left hand side of the line and then the right hand in an effort to distribute the birds evenly over the guns, giving them all a fair share of the shooting. The beaters converged on the corner of the wood and the last pheasant flew up. Reg blew the whistle and then turned to John.

"Get off as quickly as you can with the beaters; it'll soon be getting dark and it's just starting to rain. Get lined out and blank the first part through. Start as soon as you get there, don't wait for the whistle."

John followed his instructions, doing his best to keep the beaters in line as they brought the first part of the wood across. Reg was waiting on the track where they re-lined and he blew the whistle as soon as they neared him. He chivvied them along as the guns were already in place and the rain was getting heavier. The light was fading as they reached the heading of the last drive, but Reg did not hurry. John admired the way he manipulated the beaters and the pheasants, allowing the birds to fly as steadily as possible over the guns. John's fears were forgotten now as the birds flew; instead he felt both elation and satisfaction. The last few pheasants took to the wing and the final few shots were fired; a rabbit scuttled out of the last bush and raced across the field; a beater belatedly threw his stick after it and a gun raised his hat as it ran past him and into the hedge behind.

The final whistle blew and John walked towards the guns and collected up some of the pheasants; they were strewn across the ground and it looked like a battlefield. The light was fading fast and the rain was falling steadily as John helped Martin sort out the pheasants. John took little notice as he worked the feeling of comfort inside him was stronger than the outer discomfort. Reg and Fred walked over laden with pheasants, their dogs wet,

Figure 11.6   Snapshot Over the Hedge   **courtesy photo: John Tarlton**

dirty and tired at their heels.

"John, can you give Martin a hand to unload and hang up the game in the game larder?" Reg asked, adding; "I'll need nine brace for the guns — bring them up to the back kitchen of the big house and we'll have a cup of tea ready for you both."

Martin and John tied the birds as quickly as their cold wet hands allowed and then drove back to the game larder.

John unloaded while Martin hung the birds up, first on the hooks round the walls and then on some rails — he spaced them out well so that they would cool and the wet ones could dry.

"That's the lot", said John, struggling in with the last arm full! "Any ideas how many?"

"I'll have a count as soon as I've hung these up — you start along that side and then we can double check, and don't count out loud it puts me off", Martin answered.

After a few moments of silence they agreed that the total was two hundred and seventy seven pheasants, two pigeons, a woodcock and a rabbit that John knew Amber had caught.

I should think Reg would be pleased with that", Martin told him. "Come on let's go and find that cup of tea — I'm ready for it."

EVENING DISCUSSIONS

The night was cold and dark and the rain poured down. They blinked as they opened the kitchen door, the light was bright and the warmth welcomed them. Reg poured them a mug of tea each while they took off their waterproofs and left them in the porch outside.

"Here you are — here's your tea you've earned it — what's the final score?" Reg asked as they sat down at the table.

A note of pride sounded in John's voice as he announced the figure.

"Well done lad, that's not bad especially after all the trouble with that dog", Reg congratulated him. "You've not broken the record for that beat, but then you've got to have something left to aim for next year."

John sipped his hot sweet tea, it tasted good. Besides Reg and Martin with him in the kitchen were the pickers up, Fred, Ernie and Hazel and three of the older beaters. John sat back and listened as they discussed the day's shooting, how the dogs had worked, how the guns had shot and how the birds had flown.

The conversation expanded to other shoots and other keepers and John listened avidly to every word. Away in another room he could hear a roar of laughter from the guns as they shared a joke and the smell of cigar smoke wafted into the kitchen when someone opened the door. Two of the guns had already stopped by at the kitchen on their way out bidding them goodnight and offering their thanks for an enjoyable day to Reg as they discreetly pressed the folded notes into his hand as they shook it. They had thanked John as well before going on their way back to London and he had only thought to stand up as they spoke to him, when he saw Reg glance at him.

The clock on the mantlepiece chimed seven, making them realize how late it was. John was sorry when they left because he had enjoyed listening to the talk. Reg and John were the last to leave and as they did so Mr. Brinklow came in and thanked them both for a good day.

They crossed the drive to get in the landrover and John was soon brought back to the earth.

"Good day — but it's over now and it's time to think of the next one; there's a lot to do before next Saturday", Reg told him. "Could you roll the sewelling up in the morning when you're round feeding. With a bit of luck there'll be some stew waiting for us at home — let's go and find it. I'm starving."

THE CHORES

The rain was still sweeping across the fields next morning and it was a

Figure 11.7 At the End of the Day   **courtesy photo: Chas. White**

long time before it was light. John did not much enjoy the feeding, apart from the rain he saw very few pheasants; surely they could not all have been shot? He wound the sewelling up and laid it beside the track for Reg to fetch in the landrover. He was soaked through when he got home and the elation he had felt the night before had all but drained away. He saw Reg and told him how few pheasants he had seen, but Reg was not surprised and assured him that after a few days they would settle down and he would again see them on the feed rides.

John fed around again in the afternoon as the next day he would be out beating. He fetched his waterproofs to the caravan in an effort to dry them out before the morning. Reg was out as usual on the Wednesday and there was much to do on the other days in readiness for the next main day on Reg's beat.

John was up early and in contrast to the previous Saturday the morning was bright and frosty. He fed the woods he had not fed the evening before, changed and sat waiting for Reg in the landrover. John happened to remark what a lovely morning it was to Reg as he settled himself behind the steering wheel.

"Darned sunshine — the birds won't fly well in this", Reg muttered his disagreement. John sat silently beside him for the rest of the journey up to the stable yard not wishing to say anything to upset Reg further.

A START IN THE SUNSHINE

Reg's prediction about the sunshine proved right on the first two drives; the birds did not fly as well as they usually did particularly on the first drive which was off a bank. The guns were stood close to the wood and in the shade, some of the pheasants seemed not to see them at all and flew straight towards them only detecting their presence at the last moment and hastily trying to gain height again. Most of the guns made no attempt to shoot at the low birds knowing that they would make better birds another time. Half way through the morning hazy clouds began to filter across the sun so that it lost its brilliance, no longer blinding the guns or the pheasants as they faced it.

John enjoyed the day's shooting, although he worried about keeping the beaters in line, but since the number of birds in each drive were not his concern he was better able to appreciate what was happening. There were a lot of birds in every drive, but the day reached its climax with the last drive which was Reg's main pen. Never had John seen so many pheasants, as they neared the sewelling that was hung along a bank a few yards from the end of the drive which was to make the birds rise from the higher ground and make them gain more height over the guns. To John there seemed hundreds of pheasants; they stood before him their heads up confused at what was happening. They stood like chickens, a mixture of gold and black and brown on the carpet of leaves and pine needles. Flush after flush arose and the shots seemed never ending. No sooner would Reg command the line to move on, than they would have to stop as another flush of birds flew up.

The sun, like a big ball of fire slipped from view, the final whistle blew and all was quiet again.

Once again John helped Martin with the birds and willingly accepted Roger's offer to help. The stars twinkled in the dark sky and the air was frosty as they walked round to the kitchen at the back of the house and once again John enjoyed listening to the talk. The total was very nearly five hundred and for the first time for months Reg looked relaxed and the tension had gone from his face.

November was nearly ended, outside the moon shone down on the bare trees and the climax to the season had been reached.

Figure 11.8   A Shadow Dance

Season Of
Goodwill
12

DECEMBER

Figure 12.1   The Shoot Is On

SEASON OF GOODWILL

MONTH: **DECEMBER**

PHEASANTS STILL TO FEED

Reg always thought December was a dreary month, the daylight hours were few and, if the sun did not show itself, as it rarely seemed to in December, the days were dark and grey. Despite Reg and John having shot a good number of pheasants on their beats there were still a lot left in the woods and these had to be fed every day. Reg had told John that it was no longer necessary to feed the pheasants at his pen in the afternoons which was just as well as there was little enough daylight to get the other chores done.

John found that once his birds had settled down after the shoot they fed fairly consistently, whereas earlier in the season some days they had not bothered so much about coming to feed. However, now that the majority of the natural food had been eaten with the help of squirrels, pigeons and other wildlife besides the pheasants, the birds were waiting eagerly for him when he arrived to feed.

John still liked feeding each morning; he would whistle as loud as he could while he walked along the ride throwing out handfuls of grains and then he would stand quietly at the end watching and counting the birds as they came out to feed. Some would run boldly out, others would be more cautious and some would suddenly lose their nerve and run back into the cover making an acurate count difficult. Odd ones were so tame that they would feed at his feet and Sally would prick her ears forward and look quizzically at them within a few feet of her nose. Sometimes a jay or a blackbird would yell out its warning cry and the whole line of feeding pheasants would scatter back into the cover.

THE SATURDAY SHOOTS

The shoot each Saturday had now become part of the routine and John had been through every wood on the estate and was beginning to know the ground. Sometimes Reg would have to alter the way he did a drive slightly especially if it was windy. John had another good day on his beat and Reg likewise on his — after that the shoot days would be a selection of drives from either beat wherever Reg thought best to go.

Sally had come into a season soon after the main day on John's beat and so he was unable to take her for a few weeks, but now the shoot days were smaller Reg had said that she could go along. However, he still insisted that John should keep her to heel although he did suggest that if there was the chance of a very easy retrieve on a dead pheasant he could let her have it, but he was emphatic that on no account should she have a live pheasant to deal with this season. John was beginning to feel impatient about working her because she certainly seemed keen to go, but Reg was insistent and John knew if he disobeyed then he would no longer be able to take Sally out on a shoot day.

Honey and Amber were good dogs for beating and if they were an example of Reg's way of training then John thought he had best follow the advice he was offered. John had witnessed some badly behaved dogs on the shoot he went beating on and he certainly did not wish to own one like them. He had watched one day as a very disobedient labrador had run around first picking up one bird and then dropping it and picking another that it spotted. The dog would suddenly chase a runner and after that eventually catching it and returning to its owner. Before it reached him, however, the pheasant had fluttered and died in the dogs vice like grip. All the while its owner had been whistling and shouting at the animal and John could quite understand Reg's insistence that only well behaved dogs should be allowed out on a shoot.

WATCHING FOR POACHERS

The night patrols still continued, John had been out with Fred and his under-keeper besides Reg on several different occasions. He liked going with Fred because he would tell him yarns from the past and talk of the old fashioned methods of rearing when the broody hen was both incubator and brooder to the young pheasants and when all the food for the chicks had to be cooked and mixed for them.

At first John had been afraid of Fred's German Shepherd Dog, Sabre tied in the back of his pick up; she looked such a disdainful creature and the first time John had approached her Fred had quietly given her the order to speak and she had strained at the chain and bared her teeth as she barked at him.

Figure 12.2   The German Shepherd Dog (Alsation) used as a Guard Dog

Even now that John had made her acquaintance and would even dare to stroke her he still did not really like her, whereas the labradors would look into his eyes when spoken to, the German Shepherd's gaze would pierce through him making him feel uncomfortable. Fred admitted that while she was friendly enough with him, he always felt that she never quite accepted him as her master. One thing they all agreed on was that Sabre was a comfort to them on their nightly patrols and had proved in the past to be a useful deterrent when there was trouble about.

One lunchtime a keeper on the other side of the village to Reg had rung and said that he had been poached the night before and Fred too had found the tell tale signs of fresh feathers and strange footprints on the ride in one of his woods. Since then he and Reg had increased their patrols and sometimes it was two or three in the morning before John heard Reg return home.

Another evening while John was getting his tea he heard a car turn into the yard with a squeal of tyres — he looked out of the caravan door and heard Roger shouting to Reg that he had just seen an old van parked a little way off the road that divided Stonelands from Fred's estate.

"Go and get John", Reg told Roger, "I'll give Fred a ring he lives closer than we are."

Roger turned towards the caravan, but John was already half way across to him putting on his coat as he ran.

Poachers are caught

Reg was soon back out of the house and they all three climbed into the landrover and set off around the lanes at break-neck speed. Roger explained where he had seen the van and as they pulled into the track ahead of them in the headlights they could see Fred, his dog Sabre beside him on a rope snarling at two men whom Fred had confronted as they walked back to the van. One was carrying a gun, and the other three pheasants and a torch, and neither seemed inclined to argue with Fred or Sabre.

Reg asked Roger to take the landrover and phone the police and then he and John walked up to where Fred stood.

"I've sent Roger to 'phone the police", Reg told Fred. "Looks as though you've got them fair and square — John — have a look in the back of the van; here's a torch."

John took the torch from Reg and shone it through the window; in the back half covered with some old sacks was the carcass of a deer.

"There's a deer in the back", he told Reg as he walked back towards him.

Instantly one of the poachers started to explain that they had found the deer dead beside the road.

"We don't know anything about it, honest guv'nor", the other whined.

"What about those pheasants you're carrying, you don't know anything

Figure 12.3   12-Bore Shotgun and Cartridges

about them either I suppose." Fred told them: "Just shut up, we'll wait until the law get here and then you can talk."

Just then Roger pulled up in the landrover and shouted across to the group that the police were on their way.

A few minutes later a police car pulled in besides the landrover and two policemen walked over towards them and exchanged greetings with the head keepers.

"We'd better get off and finish our tea if you don't mind", Reg told Fred.

"We'll be round for a statement tomorrow", the sergeant told Reg as he turned to leave.

"O.k. you know where I live, dinner time or after dark is the best time to catch me", Reg told him as they departed and left Fred and the police to sort the matter out.

"All those nights we've all been out and those sneaking poachers have been and gone before we've gone out", Reg spoke angrily as they drove homewards. "Let's hope that they get what they deserve."

Reg turned to Roger; "Thanks for coming and so quickly; if you hadn't spotted their van we would never have caught them."

THE BOYS' DAY SHOOT

The days went by and Christmas was drawing closer. Reg had told John that he could have two or three days off over the holiday to go home, and it was up to him whether he was away for the Boxing Day shoot. This was a somewhat informal shoot which Mr. Brinklow held every year and by tradition it was the Boys' Day. Any sons of guns in the shoot or guests of Mr. Brinklow were invited and under the watchful eye of their fathers were allowed a taste of a formal day's shooting. They usually met at ten o'clock and shot through until two when everyone, including Reg and his underkeeper, adjourned to the big house for lunch. Mr. Brinklow like Reg believed that the younger generation should be taught the etiquette of the shooting field so that they should always know their manners. The day did little to add to the season's total and it was a jovial occasion.

John was undecided what to do; he wanted to be home for Christmas, but he also wanted to be out on the Boxing Day shoot. He eventually decided to go home the day before Christmas Eve and his father would bring him back early Boxing Day morning.

PREPARING FOR CHRISTMAS

The days before Christmas were hectic, yet the evenings seemed endless to John, he soon bored with reading and the television. Sometimes he and Roger would go out, but John did not much enjoy going to parties and the local pub was too posh for him to feel comfortable. He was far happier being outdoors and was impatiently looking forward to the lighter evenings. He felt an inner satisfaction when on his own in the countryside sharing the hardships of the weather and conditions just as the wild creatures did. The only pleasure John derived from the Winter, apart from it being the shooting season, was the absence of people using the footpaths. The fields and the woods were his for nearly all the farm work was centred around the farm buildings and it was seldom he saw another soul on his rounds. The visitors migrated to the countryside like birds following the sun, bringing their roaming dogs, their noisy children and their litter with them, disrupting the very peace that they came to find. John resented their presence, but at the same time sympathised with them for having to live in the towns, something he thought he would never be able to do.

Somehow the time was found to fill the corn bins and sort out the sewelling and to do all the other chores that needed doing, but, even so, John felt guilty at leaving Reg with extra work to do over the Christmas. Reg assured him that he did not mind looking after Sally and feeding his pheasants, even if they got missed one day it really would not hurt, but even so John still felt guilty.

Early Rising

He was up early the morning of his departure; he fed round and pulled up the few wires he had set after the last shoot. Mrs. Plummer took him to the station as soon as he was ready because he wanted to have time to do his Christmas shopping before he got home. There had been little opportunity to go out and he had not liked to ask for any more time off.

He had already decided to buy his parents a clock. He was not too sure about his brothers, but had thought a model kit would be a good thing for the younger one, whereas the older one he could not decide on. He had spent a long time thinking what he could get Mr. and Mrs. Plummer, but his mind was a blank. His first stop on his shopping trip was the biggest department store in town and he walked round hoping for inspiration. It came in the china department in the shape of a china pheasant. He thought that it would be suitable for both Reg and Mrs. Plummer and he knew she must like ornaments from seeing her china cabinet. He continued his way around the store, he saw a clock he thought would suit his parent's mantlepiece and bought it. Then he headed for the toy department; the model kit was easily chosen as his youngest brother was keen on aeroplanes, but still he had not thought of anything for his other brother. Suddenly he spotted some kites — yes, a kite would do and he chose one that looked like a giant bird and hoped that there would be some wind on

Christmas Day so that he might have a chance of flying it. The presents purchased he went over to the card department and chose some cards where he found a large one with pheasants in the snow on it for the Plummers. He chose some wrapping paper and then he was so laden with parcels that he wished he had brought his feed bag with him to put them all in.

Darkness had fallen and the lights from the shops, cars and street lamps shone on the wet street. He was glad when he left the hustle and bustle of the shops and the station and found a seat in the warmth of the train taking him home to the family.

Reg spent part of Christmas Day feeding the birds. Earlier he had laid in bed for a while, but had regretted it afterwards when his head began to ache and it was a relief to be outside. He had returned and enjoyed a large leisurely lunch and a sleep afterwards, but when he awoke he went outside again and did some more feeding. His son and wife and two young children were staying for the holiday and Reg found it a relief to be able to escape from the constant chatter and noise. It was dark outside by the time he had fed the dogs and given them a run and the darkness trapped him inside the house for the rest of the day.

BOXING DAY ACTIVITIES

Boxing Day morning he was eating his breakfast when he heard a car pull into the yard. He got up and opened the door to greet the visitors, calling to John and his father to come in.

"Did you have a nice Christmas?" Reg asked them — "come along in and have some breakfast, you must have left early."

"Yes, we left at half past five, but we hardly saw any other cars so we made good time. It seemed quite eerie with all the streets and roads deserted", John told him.

He excused himself and went back out to the car to fetch his bags, but not before he had walked over to the kennels and had a few words with Sally. He carried his bags back into the kitchen and put them down by the door, taking out the card and present for the Plummers. Reg and his father had stopped talking as he had come into the kitchen and he wondered what they had been saying about him.

"I've got your present — sorry it's a bit late he said to Mrs. Plummer as he handed her the gift. He watched as she opened it and hoped that she liked his choice. She showed it to Reg and then placed it carefully on the mantlepiece. John probably never realised how much she appreciated his thoughtfulness.... with sons of her own she knew how much easier it was to settle for the inevitable box of chocolates.

"Thanks", she said, "It's lovely. I'll put it in my china cupboard later on."

John sat at the table beside his father and Mrs. Plummer soon put a plateful of fried eggs, bacon and bread in front of them. She cut them off a thick wedge of bread and poured them out a mug of tea each. While they ate she went off into the sitting room to find the card and jumper that she had wrapped for John.

He opened the present when he had finished eating and he was grateful for the jumper. He had been given some shirts and socks by his family so he would not need to buy much in the way of clothing during the coming year — a job which he loathed.

"Well, did you get anything nice for Christmas?", Mrs. Plummer asked him after he had thanked her for the jumper.

"Yes, Mum and Dad gave me a Twelve Bore — it's for my birthday as well and my brothers gave me some cartridges. I had some shirts and socks as well so I'm well stocked up now", John answered.

"That'll be better than that old Four-ten you've got", Reg told him.

They finished a second mug of tea each and John's father took his leave, saying that if he did not get off soon he would be late visiting his relations although secretly he would have preferred to miss the visit.

John and Reg arrived in the stable yard at a quarter to ten and Reg had explained the plans for the day to him while driving up to the big house. John was surprised how few beaters had turned up and how many people were standing about in the front drive. Indeed, there were many more of them than there were beaters.

"Get the beaters loaded up", Reg told him before walking through the archway towards the waiting crowd. A few minutes later he returned with an assortment of volunteer beaters. There was a variety of women and children dressed in all manner of clothing and their ages ranged from six to sixty.

John gave Roger a nudge:

"What are that lot doing?" he asked.

"They're the beaters — no one wants to turn out on Boxing Day so by tradition wives, sisters and, by the look of that one there, grannies turn out in line — didn't Reg tell you?" laughed Roger.

John tried not to stare at them as they sat on the trailer, their upper class voices ringing out across the fields in the crisp morning air, warning all pheasants of their imminent arrival. John looked across at Reg who seemed quite placid despite the rabble.

The trailer pulled off the track and the passengers got off. The first necessity was to cut sticks for the new beaters and several minutes elapsed before Reg had the slightest semblance of order; eventually they were ready and Reg blew the whistle. He expected the women and children to push their way through the bushes just as the proper beaters did. John was surprised at how hard Reg dared to be with them and equally how willingly they tackled the brambles despite their lack of proper clothing — secretly John thought they must be mad to spend Boxing Day in such a manner. The dogs they had brought with them were a slight problem until Reg instructed they should all be kept on the lead, which must have made beating even more difficult for their owners. John and Reg laughed to each other when they saw one woman had armed herself with what looked like a washing line so that her dog could still run around while it was on the lead. John visualised what would happen if the dog chased after a rabbit in one of the thick plantations.

The line moved towards the end of the drive in zig-zag fashion because Reg and John had almost given up trying to keep a straight line. Several birds rose into the air at once and a barrage of shot greeted them, all but one continued their uninterrupted flight to the next wood.

They had completed five drives before Mr. Brinklow called a halt. The total bag was only seventeen pheasants, but John had developed a sneaking admiration for the way the women and children had survived the morning. They even appeared to have enjoyed themselves despite the unaccustomed exercise and the thickness of the cover that Reg had sent them through.

INTRODUCTION TO THE SHOOT ROOM

They climbed onto the trailer and rode back to the stable yard. Soon they were all crowded into the shoot room enjoying the warmth from the big log fire and their gin and tonics or lemonade. Mrs. Plummer had helped Mrs. Brinklow prepare the meal and John hungrily glanced at the laden table as he found himself a chair in the corner.

He had never been inside the shoot room before and he suddenly felt self conscious as he tried to shrink into the corner. He sat back and absorbed the atmosphere, the huge oval table, the wood panelling and the blazing log fire made it look like a Christmas card scene from a byegone age. The walls were hung with sporting pictures — hunting, shooting and fishing and, over the fireplace, was a fine set of red deer antlers with a plaque underneath bearing the place and date where it had been shot. In between the pictures on the walls were the much smaller antlers of roe deer, each mounted on a wooden shield and each bearing a similar plaque to the red deer antlers. These were trophies from Mr. Brinklow's stalking expeditions; some were from Stonelands and some from Scotland. Hung beneath the antlers over the fireplace was an ancient Damascus barrelled hammer gun which had belonged to Mr. Brinklow's grandfather. The room was crowded and everyone was talking, the smell of cigars intermingled with the wood smoke from the fire.

Reg edged his way between the people and came towards John, a glass in each hand.

"You all right lad? — I see you've found yourself a corner — good idea. I've brought you a beer I expect you're as thirsty as I am after all that shouting at the beaters — I'm glad we don't have that lot every week."

"I expect you would either have trained them or sacked them by now if you did", John answered.

"Or handed in my notice", Reg added — he looked round and saw his wife carrying in a huge bowl filled with steaming baked potatoes.

"Looks as though it's grub time — I'm starving, it's been a long morning."

John and Reg joined the end of the queue and piled their plates high with the cold meat, salads, pickles and hot potatoes when their turn came. They made their way back to their chairs in the corner and started to eat. Mr. Brinklow came over to them and asked if they were alright, and then disappeared back into the crowd. One of the regular guns came over and chatted to them while they ate, he seemed more concerned with the large gin and tonic he was enjoying than acquiring a plate full of food. He was an elderly man and John knew that he had been shooting at Stonelands before Reg had started there. He talked quite a lot to John and John was soon chatting back, his shyness forgotten.

The plates were stacked away, the glasses refilled and even bigger cigars were lit. Reg and John stayed seated in the corner and several people came over to talk to Reg so that they were not alone. They talked of old acquaintances and shoots and John sat quietly listening. Occasionally one of the boys who had been shooting would, on their father's instructions, come over and discreetly press their tip into Reg's hand just as their fathers would do if they had been the guest.

Slowly the room became less crowded as the guests dispersed. Reg stood up to leave and Mr. Brinklow came over to thank him and press some more notes into the head keeper's hand. He thanked John as well and to his surprise he pressed some notes into his hand explaining that it was his Christmas box.

They stopped by the kitchen on the way out to thank Mrs. Brinklow for the food and to see if Mrs. Plummer was ready to leave.

Outside it was cold and dark and quiet and ice had already formed on the windscreen of the landrover as they climbed into it.

AN INVITATION TO THE PLUMMERS

"Would you like to come round for tea", Mrs. Plummer asked John.

"Yes please, I'd love to. It'll seem rather quiet in the caravan tonight after the last few days. I'll see to Sally and get changed first", he answered.

"Good — you come round as soon as you are ready. My son and his family are staying — you've not met him yet have you?"

"No, I haven't", John answered and then turning to Reg asked him:

"Would you like me to feed your dogs?"

"Yes, if you would", Reg replied.

John fed the dogs and washed and changed before joining the Plummers. He was soon ushered into an armchair beside Reg in front of the blazing fire. Mrs. Plummer brought him in a cup of tea.

"There's nothing better than a good cup of tea, I'm not too keen on all that boozing at lunchtime it always gives me a headache", Reg remarked.

John siped the hot tea and he felt his face glow in the warmth of the fire. Reg's son joined them and they were soon chatting while the children played on the floor with their toys and the womanfolk prepared tea.

THE NEW YEAR

Christmas was no sooner over than the New Year was upon them. Roger had organised a party and luckily as it turned out the guns had no wish to shoot on New Years Day so John was able to enjoy the party without the thought of having to get up early.

Roger had not only asked John and his other friends but anyone on the estate who wanted to go. Reg had declined the invitation, but several of the others had accepted and for John it was the first proper opportunity he had to meet some of them. He found them difficult to recognise in their smart clothes and it amused John to discover how much some of them enjoyed themselves. Martin and his partner had done the twist with so much enthusiasm that everyone else had stood back and given them a round of applause when the record ended.

Everybody had brought some drink with them and the girls had prepared some food and John soon found that this was one party that he did enjoy.

The television was turned on a few minutes before midnight and as Big Ben chimed the hour everyone crossed arms and sang Auld Lang Syne. They refilled their glasses, put on another record and continued with the party.

John left at two o'clock, he was one of the first to leave and the party was still in full swing.

He walked down the lane in the dark and the cold air instead of making him feel better as he had hoped made him feel worse, he felt dizzy and he wished he was already in bed. He opened and closed the gate quietly and tried to creep past the kennels, but he accidently kicked a bucket that had been left beside the shed and the dogs rushed out barking. John crept on towards the caravan wishing they would be quiet and hoping that Reg hadn't heard them and if he had, that he had not known what they were barking at.

Figure 12.4   A Poacher at Bay

A Special
Shoot
13

JANUARY

Figure 13.1 The Author when the Shoot is Over **(courtesy photo: Chas. White)**

A SPECIAL SHOOT

MONTH: JANUARY

THE HANGOVER

John turned over in bed and opened one eye, he looked at the clock — he had overslept. Sitting up quickly he discovered that he still had his clothes on, his head throbbed and he gently laid down again. He laid there for several minutes delaying the uncomfortable process of attaining a vertical position. Eventually he crept over to the kettle and switched it on — had it been such an enjoyable evening he wondered. The strong sweet coffee did little to improve his headache and, later, when he left the caravan Reg watched him from the shed, a wry grin on his face as he recalled similar mornings of his youth. Reg had heard John disturb the dogs on his way back in the early hours of the morning and was not surprised when he saw the wilting figure step out from the caravan an hour later than usual. The memories of his own youth were still too fresh in his mind for him to feel angry with the boy. The lad's hangover would be sufficient punishment.

GETTING BACK TO NORMAL

After the Boxing Day shoot John found it pleasant to get back to normal with the usual team of beaters. There were only three shoots left in January and he suddenly realised how quickly the season had passed. The bags were obviously smaller now and the days seemed more relaxed. The last day of all the guns would only be allowed to shoot cocks, but until then Reg requested that they should take cocks in preference to hens and John noticed that several of the guns hardly shot at a hen on these days.

John still kept Sally close to him when beating, but if he saw that she had winded a pheasant close by he would let her put it up, telling her to 'leave it' the moment it moved and never letting her get more than a few feet away from him. He had let her retrieve the odd dead pheasants that had lain out in the field after the drives, but had not hunted her after runners or with the other dogs. She was still obedient and John did not often have to correct her and, even then, the sharp tone of his voice was often enough to stop her.

In mid-January the wind had settled into the North East and for days it blew strongly so that the ground was kept frozen hard: It was easier to walk on the frozen ground but was very uncomfortable where it had frozen the hoof prints or knobbly ground. John disliked the cold wind; Reg called it 'lazy' because it blew straight through the body rather than go round it. The pheasants that had survived the shooting were hungry now and would come running up as soon as they heard his whistle. Hordes of smaller birds would also join the pheasants on the feed ride; there were robins, blackbirds, chaffinches and tits and even a rabbit came regularly out to feed in one wood. Squirrels and an occasional rat would join the birds, all of them grateful for the grain when the frozen ground made finding enough food to keep alive difficult. John had not set his snares and traps after Christmas; but he did put a trap in each corn bin and was surprised at the number of squirrels he had caught in them.

THE COCK DAY

The **cock day** was nearly a disaster and from the start nothing seemed to go right. The night before it had rained and the bitter cold wind had frozen it

Figure 13.2   Winter Feed Ride

so that every road in the vicinity was like a skating rink. Some of the guns and some of the beaters were late arriving and told grisly tales of ambulance and police dealing with accidents at different places along the roads leading to Stonelands. When eventually they did start the shoot one gun, through some misunderstanding, shot hens and for the first time John saw Reg really angry. It was all the head keeper could do to remember his manners and he was very soon hurrying towards Mr. Brinklow at the end of the drive.

Later in the morning one of the gun's dogs ran into the drive and put several pheasants back over the beaters before its embarassed owner could persuade it to return to him.

On the drive before lunch, Fred's pick up slid off the track and into a ditch so that Martin and his tractor had to be dispatched to tow it out. Fortunately little damage was done to the truck but it meant a very short lunch break for those concerned.

After lunch the sky darkened and a mixture of rain and sleet swept across the fields numbing the feet and hands in the unpleasant conditions and evoking a unanimous decision to cancel the last drive.

After the final day for the syndicate Reg was allowed to organize another cock day to which he invited his friends and those who had helped him on the other shoot days, it was a way of thanking them for their hard work for a minimal wage on the Saturdays throughout the season.

Mr. Brinklow came out shooting on this day, but only because Reg asked him to and he was expected to beat through when his turn came. John was surprised how seriously Reg took the day and it was run with similar precision as the proper shoot days.

They all met in the stable yard and Reg divided them into two groups, each group drew for numbers just as the syndicate guns did. One team would then stand for the first drive while the other team acted as beaters and then they would change over. Reg and John beat all day, but the others all had alternate drives as standing guns. Reg was very strict about discipline and **no one who was beating was allowed to shoot a pheasant that flew forward towards the waiting guns.** One of the beaters in the heat of the moment had shot at a cock that was not very high over John; the shots splattered through the trees and the pheasant nearly landed on top of John's head. Reg saw the incident and even though no harm was done he rated the person in question and warned him that if it happened again on the next drive, he would be sent home.

John had left Sally at home much to her indignation, but Reg had warned him that the temptation to do wrong would be too great on such a day so it seemed sensible not to bring her. He had taken his new gun and had several shots ending the day with two cocks and a squirrel to his credit, but declining to admit how many shots he had fired. He enjoyed the day, but it was tinged with sadness that this was the last shoot day of the season for him. Reg still had two days out, one at Fred's place and one at his friends in Hampshire, but for John it was the finish.

Everybody got off the trailer in the stable yard and stowed their guns and waterproofs away into their assorted vehicles. Goodbyes and thanks were said, for many of them would not meet up again until the start of the next season, they came from many walks of life besides being farm workers. Several spent their working lives sitting behind a desk and they enjoyed the shooting season as a reason to be outside and getting some much needed exercise through the winter months.

REFLECTIONS OF THE YEAR

A few of Reg's closer friends went back to his house for a meal and John had taken his leave and was in bed long before the last one departed. He felt a little depressed as he lay in bed thinking over the day. He would miss the company, the jokes and the stories. During the last few months he had listened a lot and had learned to differentiate between the stories that were true and the ones that were exaggerated. He disregarded the ones who bragged and talked too much, but listened eagerly to the men who were genuine, continually thirsting for more knowledge. Reg had watched the boy, grateful that he was not turning out like some he had known who were of the opinion that having done the job for a year they knew all about it. He was grateful too that John could be trusted and so that he may even have the chance to enjoy a holiday with his wife this year, now that there was somebody responsible enough to look after things in his absence.

The Season
Ends
14

Figure 14.1   On the Alert

THE SEASON ENDS

AN ANTI-CLIMAX

With the shooting over, the next task for John was to prepare for catching up, and so the year had turned full cycle. He thought as he started to sort out the catchers that he had completed one revolution in the tread mill and he wondered how many more he would complete in his life. Once he had caught up his share of the hens needed he would be able to have a couple of weeks holiday and already he was looking forward to some ferreting with old Tom the keeper near his home.

John felt the end of the season was an anti-climax in that it all suddenly finished. He envied Reg the opportunity of the last day of the season out. Reg had often talked of his friend in Hampshire and he had come to Stonelands on the cock day, but with so many people there that John knew he had no chance to meet him properly. Reg only saw Peter occasionally, but they had once keepered on neighbouring estates and had continued their friendship despite living miles apart. They usually went to each others cock days and Reg would go over to the hare shoot that his friend organised. There were few hares at Stonelands and it was difficult for John to imagine that it was possible to shoot two or three hundred in one day on some estates.

A WELCOME INVITATION

Reg had already instructed John what work he wanted done during his absence the following day and John was surprised when he knocked on the caravan door later in the evening.

"My friend Peter, the one in Hampshire has just rung up and said that three of the people he had asked shooting tomorrow have gone down with 'flu, he wondered if you'd like to go", Reg explained.

"Cor — yes — can I really", John answered his face beaming.

Reg smiled at the excitement in the boy's voice — "It'll be a good day", he continued. "They usually get about one hundred and fifty cocks and his wife lays on lunch and some tea when we've finished. Usually a few of us end up at the local so it'll be quite a day. Don't bother to do up any grub, I'll take a large flask of coffee that will do for both of us. You're lucky to be asked on a day like that. By the way, don't believe all they'll tell you about me. I started off on the neighbouring estate when I was your age. I was there for five years and some of those old keepers won't ever let me forget my mistakes."

Reg turned to leave "I'll pick you up at seven sharp."

"Thanks ever so much", John called after him, knowing that it had really been up to Reg whether he had been able to go or not.

It was still dark the next morning as Reg and John loaded their gear into the landrover. They loaded their guns, cartridges, wellingtons and waterproofs in the back and Honey jumped in amongst it all. Reg fastened the tail gate shut and the canvas back tight down. John climbed into the front alongside Reg; a fine drizzle smeared the windscreen as they set off down the lane. The sky slowly lightened behind them as they headed westward, the rough grass downland gave way to the gentler rolling downs of West Sussex and then the big open fields of Hampshire. The drizzle faded with the darkness and the morning brightened although the sun lacked sufficient strength to break through the clouds. John looked about him, taking in the changing scenery.

"Nearly there", Reg's voice broke through the monotonous throbbing of the diesel engine.

They turned off the main road and drove along steep banked roads flanked with yew and gigantic old beech trees. The chalk and flints glistened white against the wet earth.

Reg turned off the lane and up a flinty track and pulled up beside a barn. A little way off John could see a house and he presumed it to be where Peter lived. Reg reached into the basket by John's feet and pulled out the flask.

"I think there's a bit of cake each in there if you're hungry", Reg told him as he poured out the coffee.

John was grateful for the large slice of fruit cake and the hot coffee — breakfast seemed an age ago. Other cars began to arrive in the yard and several men came over to Reg and had a word with him. Peter walked over and greeted Reg as well.

"Glad you could come John", he said peering in the window beside Reg.

"Thanks very much for asking me", John replied.

"We'll be moving off soon, nearly everybody is here now", Peter told Reg.

John quickly drank the remainder of his coffee and then he and Reg got out and went round the back of the landrover. Honey was pleased when they opened the back and let her out. She joined the throng of dogs, several of whom came up and sniffed her. She curled her lip up at them, but they continued their investigations.

John and Reg hastily put on their wellingtons and waterproofs and joined the group surrounding Peter. He was reading from a list he had written of the names of the people he had asked. He first called out three names of the men who would be captains of each team and then the others he divided into three teams. John was relieved to hear his name called along with Regs' so at least he knew one person in his team. Each team then drew the numbers for their pegs for the first drive. There would be two teams beating for each drive and one standing forward. The captains drew for who would stand first and so it was that John found himself standing at a peg with pheasants being driven towards him for the first time in his life. He felt very self-conscious, especially after he had missed two cocks flying straight over him, he felt even worse when a small flush got up near the end of the drive and he panicked, not knowing which bird to aim at and eventually only firing one barrel and having no time to fire the second. The beaters were stepping over the fence at the end of the drive when a cock bird suddenly burst from the dead grass round one of the fence posts and hurtled towards John. He was quite unprepared for it but he snapped his gun shut, raised it and pulled the trigger, to his amazement it crumpled in mid air and landed near his feet amidst a cheer from the entire company.

Analysing what had happened later he decided that he had missed the first two easy ones because he had watched them coming towards him for so long. He had time to think about aiming and firing so that it was not a natural response. Later he had missed the third chance simply because he had spent too much time trying to decide which bird to take so that he left it too late. The last one he had hit purely because it caught him by surprise and he had responded automatically without having time to think. Reg agreed with his theory when they discussed it. Having shot a pheasant John felt a lot less nervous. His confidence had grown and he relaxed and began to enjoy himself.

The two teams whose turn it was to beat for the second drive climbed up on the trailer to take them there and before long John was talking to some of the men. The older ones were soon telling him stories of Reg's younger days in voices that they judged loud enough for Reg to hear. One old man who was a very agile seventy delighted in regaling John with tales of Reg's misdemeanours, his eyes twinkled from his weather beaten face and his grin displayed toothless gums. John saw Reg looking in his direction several times and in the end he could no longer resist the temptation to wink at Reg, no doubt adding to Reg's concern as to what lies the old codger was filling John's head with, for he well remembered the old man's wicked sense of humour.

John looked about him as they drove along. The shoot was totally different to Stonelands. The latter had large woods and a lot of forestry, this estate had smaller woods and more hedges, the fields were larger and the ground was littered with flints of varying sizes. Where rabbits had scraped out holes, knobs of chalk were piled high – it was pure chalk with no soil or

Figure 14.2   Old Man's Beard Amongst Yew and Silver Birch

flints mixed in and it shone white in the darkness of the yew trees. The yew trees, where they grew thickly, formed a canopy that little light could penetrate and the ground below them was bare. Great beech trees flourished, their rich brown leaves still lay thick on the ground beneath. Ash, sycamore and hazel grew interlaced with the fibrous trailing branches of old man's beard, it's cotton wool like seeds showing white amidst the dark bare branches. John took an instant dislike to old man's beard, even the thinnest pieces would not break and it was very nearly impossible to push a way through the patches of it. John would not have been at all surprised to see Tarzan come swinging through the trees on one of the rope like branches.

A DIVERSION WITH OLD JACK

The fourth drive was Reg and John's turn to stand again and there was only a short distance to walk from the end of the previous drive. They had been instructed to line up a track through the wood and as they walked up to their pegs John could see behind them a thin haze of smoke.

"Come on John we'll have about ten minutes to wait, let's go and see old Jack," Reg suggested.

They walked across a clearing towards an old canvas and wattle structure, in front of it was an old man hard at work. Piles of hazel sticks were stacked around and in a rail were lodged six bill hooks, every one worn to half its original size by years of sharpening. The air smelled of wood smoke as John watched the old man as he wove the thin hazel sticks in and out of the uprights, his hard strong hands twisting the hazel and forcing it down tight, aided every now and then by him kneeling on it. He stopped briefly when Reg spoke to him, then moved over to the rail and picked up a bill hook and a long hazel stick. The two men talked and John watched old Jack deftly split the thin hazel sticks. He seldom looked at what he was doing, his thick hands were sensitive to the nature of the wood and a slight twist with the bill hook was enough to ensure that it split evenly.

John marvelled at the skill of the old man and how easy he made it look. When he had split enough sticks he resumed weaving them again forming a wattle hurdle the kind of which had been used for decades. A life time's experience made the work second nature to him and he was as much a part of the wood as the hazel he worked with. His entire life had been spent coppicing and hurdle making as had his father and grandfather before him, but now it would soon end because neither of his sons had chosen to follow him.

A shot rang out causing Reg to bid the old man a hasty goodbye and they hurried back to their pegs. John glanced back at the scene and thought he

Figure 14.3   The Old Hurdle Maker — a Dying Breed

would never forget it. The old man working in the clearing surrounded by growing hazel of varying height where he had harvested it in different years. There were patches of bramble and tall dry teazles that had taken advantage of the extra light and already a stunted primrose flowered nearby. The smell of wood smoke and the sound of the old man working jolted his emotions and he felt he was looking into the past, for no future that he could visualise would have a place for a hurdle maker in it. A cock pheasant clattered up and sailed over the trees above his neighbours head and John's thoughts were instantly dismissed.

LUNCH TIME AND A NEW START

They all sat on straw bales in the barn while they ate their lunch, Peter's wife brought out steaming hot soup, thick crusty bread and cheese and pickles washed down with cans of beer. There were hot mince pies to follow and seldom thought John, had food tasted better.

Soon they were outside again and back to the business in hand. John's shooting improved during the day, but he knew that it would be a long time before he would attain the smooth unhurried action that Reg applied with such deadly precision.

Darkness fell as they finished the last drive behind Peter's house and when all the birds had been picked up they made their way back to the barn. Reg and John stripped off their waterproofs, changed their wellingtons and put their guns back into the slips and loaded everything into the back of the landrover with Honey, who, despite Reg's cursing, raked the coats into a pile with her front paw and curled up comfortably on top of them, tired after her day's work.

THE SHARE OUT

Peter laid the braces of pheasants on the ground alongside the barn, a few hen birds showed obviously amongst the cocks, but only one person would admit to shooting one, quite by accident. The rest were attributed to the dogs. The total was one hundred and sixty pheasants, several rabbits, pigeons, squirrels and jays. John had not added greatly to the bag, but he knew that Reg had probably made up for that.

"Help yourself to a brace each and then come and have a cup of tea in the barn," Peter shouted.

Reg and John each took a brace, Reg slyly choosing a brace of hens because he knew they were nicer to eat and that they would very likely have no shot in them if they had been caught by the dogs. He laid the birds in the spare wheel on the bonnet of the landrover reminding John that he should never put the pheasants in with a dog as there was always the chance it may decide to eat them.

They returned to the barn where they ate their fill of sandwiches, sausage rolls and cake and quenched their thirst with mugs of tea.

Most of them left when they had finished tea leaving a few of Peter's friends and at his suggestion they adjourned to his kitchen where he produced a bottle of whisky. The room was warm and homely and once again John enjoyed listening to stories of shoots and shooting; of keepers and dogs. They exchanged news of mutual acquaintances and talked of the day's shooting and, as usual, John said little and learned much. He sipped the whisky Peter had handed him but the amber fluid burned his mouth and he did not enjoy it. A few more men went until there were only three left besides Reg and John; Peter and his young under-keeper Jim. Peter suggested that they should visit their local pub and so they took their cars and landrovers along the lane to the pub.

A SOCIAL AT THE VILLAGE PUB

John looked about him as he followed the men in. The bar was a complete contrast to the pubs in the village near Stonelands where the thick carpets and phoney antiques attracted town dwellers. Under his feet were rafia mats covering the worn tiled floor, a fire blazed in the brick hearth and either side of the scrubbed tables were wooden benches. The bar was dark wood and the glasses and bottles were stacked neatly on the shelves behind and John thought that the room had probably not altered since Reg had left the area.

Figure 14-4   The Pub from an Old Scene.

The landlord was an old man, his body and hands twisted with arthritis, but his eyes twinkled when he saw the keepers and his dry wit soon became apparent. John looked around again and thought that this was how a country pub should be. The wooden furniture was plain and simple and he felt at ease in the natural surroundings; the pubs near Stonelands were full of plastic and the synthetic atmosphere left him uncomfortable.

The only other customers in the pub were two old men sitting in a corner absorbed with playing dominoes and smoking their pipes.

The keepers settled on stools along the bar and soon the landlord was reliving his younger days when he had loaded on big estates, days when they had bags reaching four figures and every guest had shot with two guns and a loader whose job it was to take the empty gun, reload it and hold it in readiness for him to take. The talk inevitably turned to the war and in particular the Home Guard; the landlord's tales of how the Home Guard, whose headquarters were four miles distant in the local village, had for some inexplicable reason been moved to the barn opposite his pub which was miles from anywhere and of how one member of which had been asked what he would do if he saw the Germans while he was on duty answered that he would go and fetch the local squire!! The old landlord's eyes twinkled even more when he remembered the local parson who held the Harvest Festival in the pub because he would have a larger congregation and of the time when the parson had called by and ordered ginger beer to which the Landlord had secretly added vodka. John listened as the tales continued, a few more local country folk came in and it was not long before the singing started.

The landlord left his long suffering wife to mind the bar and he joined the keepers, his deep strong voice belied the frailness of his body as he led the singing starting with an old country song:

> **Now I got grumpy and cross**
> **T'other day when the boss**
> **said I were getting too old to employ**
> **Tho' I aint come to harm**
> **Tho' I worked on his farm**
> **Nigh fifty seven years man and boy.**
> **Surely times would be hard**
> **If from work I be barred**
> **And the missus t'would worry her too**
> **So the gaffer I sees**
> **And I said if you please**
> **Would you find I a light job to do**
> **For I be too old to mow**
> **And I be too old to sow**

I shall be ninety seven next year
Tho' I still like a smoke
And I still like a glass of good beer
So the gaffer were kind and a job he did find
And he paid I two shillings a day
For it don't need much sense
I just sits on the fence
A scarin the crows away
I've a wife kind and true
And a boy of seventy two
Who do help keep the wolf from the door.
I've a roof o'er my head
And a nice comfy bed
So what do a fella want more
And when they put I below
To my job I shall go
A scarin the crows away

Everyone joined in with the last line and the landlord lifted the flap in the bar and walked through, Reg looked at his watch.

"We'd better get off", he said to John "the missus will be wondering where we've got to, not that she expects me home early when I get in this bad company", the last remark he spoke loudly enough for his friends to hear.

"Aye, things ain't altered much in this neck of the woods", one of his friends answered. "Closing time here is when the last customer goes home — ain't that right landlord?"

The landlord kept a straight face as he set about refilling their glasses and declined to answer.

"Not for us — we must get off", Reg told him.

THE RETURN JOURNEY

The air was cold; they stepped outside, the sky had cleared and the stars shone frostily in the black sky. Soon they were drumming along the roads towards home.

"Won't Mrs. Plummer be worrying where we've got to?" asked John.

"No, she knows I'll be late and she said she'd see to the dogs — she knows better than to expect me home early when I get with that crowd — I hadn't realised it was quite so late — the time soon goes when you're enjoying yourself", Reg answered.

John had to agree with the last remark because the day had gone too quickly and he had certainly enjoyed himself. They talked for a while about the keepers that John had met that day and about the old hurdle maker. Old Jack had been cutting hazel on the estate before Reg had been born. He would work all day alone in the woods and besides the hurdles he would make bird tables and tie up bundles of pea sticks and bean sticks. He also cut thousands of short spars that were used by thatchers, his work was always in demand and yet with no-one to follow him who would there be to fulfill the need? Few youngsters were interested in the craft or would have the patience to spend years learning it, and yet like that of the thatcher there was a continual demand for the work.

Reg remarked how over the years that he had known the estate it had changed. Every January when he visited there were more hedges gone and cottages sold off, it saddened him and he knew that if it was not for the high price that rich people would pay to rent a shoot there would probably be no hedges and no woods at all on the place, the whole estate would be one prairie-like-field and Reg thought that people who wanted to ban shooting should always remember that. The old woodlands and hedges would have no value to the estate unless they could be let for shooting. Gone were the days when men worked for a fair living, few seemed content with that any more, profit was the word on the lips of people these days and the hurdle maker and the publican were a dying breed.

The continual drumming and the warmth of the landrover soon lulled John to sleep and it was not until Reg turned sharply into his drive that he awoke.

Reg breathed a sigh of relief to be home, it was a long tiring drive, but he would not have missed his day out. They unloaded the landrover and fed Honey before shutting her back in the kennel. Amber came out to greet her apprehensively; she sniffed Honey all over even to the tip of her tail before she would allow her into the kennel.

A YEAR COMPLETED

John collected his gear and thanked Reg for his day out — never had he enjoyed a day so much and as he sat in the caravan sipping a mug of hot coffee he thought back over the day. His watch ticked its way past midnight and the date on it altered to the second of February. He had been at Stonelands exactly a year. His thoughts turned back to when Reg had met him at the station that first time and he realised how green he had been and how patiently Reg suffered his mistakes and shared with him the knowledge that he had acquired over the years. Nature was a fickle creature and any man that worked with her for a companion could never truthfully say that he knew all there was to know.

It was long past midnight before John climbed into bed and as he drifted off to sleep he dreamt that Reg was banging on the caravan door shouting that he ought to be up and outside by now — or was it morning already!

APPENDIX

SOME USEFUL FACTS FOR GAMEKEEPERS

APPENDIX

INFORMATION

Some excellent advisory booklets are published by **The Game Conservancy** and can be obtained from their headquarters at Fordingbridge in Hampshire. A wide variety of topics are covered and include Pheasant and Partridge egg production, Incubation and Hatching; Diseases of Game Birds and Wildfowl; and Pheasant Rearing.

SHOOTING SEASONS IN GREAT BRITAIN
(All dates inclusive)

Grouse	August 12 — December 10
Partridge	September 1 — February 1
Pheasant	October 1 — February 1
Snipe	August 12 — January 31
Wild duck and Geese	September 1 — January 31
Woodcock	October 1 — January 31 (England and Wales) September 1 — January 31 (Scotland)

In Great Britain it is illegal to shoot any of the above on Sundays or on Christmas Day except in a few prescribed areas.

INCUBATORS

The 24 day incubation period of pheasant eggs is divided into two phases, the 'setting' period which is the first 21 days and the 'hatching' period of the last 3 days. A temperature of approximately 100⁰ F or 37⁰ C must be maintained and a 60-70% hatch of all eggs set is satisfactory. A list of some incubators in use is given below; some give better results than others.

Western	**Primula**
Hamer	**Eltex**
Ironclad	**Agri**
Bristol	**Brinsea**
Marsh	**Covattutto**
Glevum	**Eyles**
Concord	**Hovabator**
Jennings	**Vision**
Papworth	**Victoria**

The day old pheasant chick requires a brooder temperature of 100F or 37C to begin with. This should be slowly reduced so that at 4-5 weeks old the chicks are without heat during the day and at six weeks of age are completely off heat. Gas, electric or paraffin heaters can be used but avoid any giving off a lot of light after the first few days as this can cause feather pecking.

FEEDING

The pheasant chick has similar nutritional requirements to that of a turkey chick and turkey rations can be used successfully. However, many firms now produce specially formulated food for pheasants incorporating low levels of certain drugs to combat disease. These feeds can be divided roughly into five categories; the protein levels stated are approximate:

Breeders Pellets 18% protein for breeding stock.

Chick Crumbs 25% protein for chicks day old to 2-3 weeks.

Rearing Pellets 21% protein for poults 3 to 5 or 6 weeks.

Grower Pellets 18% protein for poults 5 to 8 weeks.

Covert Pellets 16% protein for poults 8 weeks and over.

Wheat is generally used to feed older poults and mature birds; sometimes whole or kibbled maize is added and small amounts of barley and oats can also be used.